HOW TO START RALLYING
Colin Malkin

as told to Richard Hudson-Evans

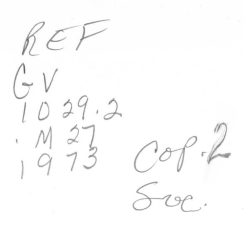

1st Impression February 1970
2nd Impression August 1970
3rd Impression November 1973

Parts of this book first appeared in Cars and Car
Conversions as a series entitled
Come Rallying as told to Richard Hudson-Evans
by Colin Malkin.
Here the information has been updated and increased.

ISBN 0 85113 0240

Published by
Speedsport Motobooks
Bercourt House, York Road, Brentford,
Middlesex, TW8 0QP, England.

Printed in Great Britain by
HGA Printing Company Limited
Brentford, Middlesex

contents

The Cockerill/Binns MGB GT is pursued through the unbelievable winter scenery of the Greystokes stage in the '69 RAC Rally.

INTRODUCTION

COLIN Malkin swept all before him in 1968 in British Rallying. The British Trials and Rally Drivers' Association Gold Star, RAC Rally Championship and The Motoring News Rally Championship all fell to Colin's winning formula.

Essential ingredients to success were a works prepared Hillman Imp, which seemed to have evolved into an almost indestructible rally chariot, and the skilful direction of John Brown.

At twenty-six, Colin has packed a variety of competition experience behind him. Starting off in earnest by passing his test the day after his seventeenth birthday, he propelled what must surely be the number one trainer car— Morris Minor. Needless to say, an over-enthusiastic debut on a local rally terminated with a roll. An A40 followed the Minor—to the same expensive fate. So it had to be a spell in the navigator's seat. During this invaluable introduction into seeing other people's mistakes at close quarters, as well as their misfortunes, Colin was accumulating the most essential asset of any aspiring rallyist—Rallymanship.

However, the call of the steering wheel became too much. The ex-Fitzpatrick Mini was acquired, and in full-racer condition it made a startling sortie on the Nutcracker. On the infamous Farmers road, this 1293 ended as quickly as it had started—in a heap of scrap.

But Colin had now been too deeply bitten to pull out. So one very evil—and exceedingly tatty—850 was discovered lurking at the back of an auction room. On the exchange of £50 the desirable carriage was his, and it didn't take him very long to transform it into a 1293 "S". On the next Welsh International Colin brought this Min home in sixth overall. He had arrived !

Based then at his garage in Kenilworth, Colin found that the sport was taking up more and more of his time. The '66 Circuit of Ireland marked the next step in the right direction : he was loaned a 998 Imp from Rootes Competition Department. He rewarded their trust in his ability with a splendid seventh overall and was the first Rootes driver to finish. From this point on there could be no more Minis, so an Imp was bought for the home Nationals —a logical thing to do, as he was then selling Rootes cars from his showroom. The car very quickly found its way into works-replica trim, by way of the Competition Department.

Success somehow seemed to elude him until the next Welsh International. Despite suffering severe frontal damage on the way to the start, a consistent run brought tenth place.

The family

The Malkin family all used to be tied up with the motor trade and competing in motoring events. His late father was a quick rallyman, so there was always plenty of encouragement for all juniors to dabble in the noble art. Both his brothers, Keith and Barrie, used to autocross regularly and Colin was a regular award winner himself, in a Mini and a Lotus 6. But it was circuit racing at which he excelled.

He thought of using a Diva 1500, but, amazingly, found it far too fast at the time. So a Lotus 7 was bought from Roy Lane. This car started life as a Lotus II, and still maintained its De Dion rear end as well as a dry sump BMC "A" motor. In this car Colin won six races out of eight starts and broke two lap records.

For the RAC-that-never-was, his Californian demonstrator was brought into service, albeit with suitable works goodies. So when rallying recommenced this was already in the wardrobe. His win on the all-special stage Bristowe started his winning streak.

It was at this stage, before the season had really got under way, that Colin teamed up with John Brown. They entered the Circuit but, when a bottom pulley came away, their rally was run. Needless to say the Californian was climbing up the leader board at the time. It was shortly after this that the car was finished off in a road accident.

A full works car was provided for the Scottish, and gave Colin one of his finest drives. It was a very close thing between Ytterbring and Colin for second and third spots, but punctures decided the final order. Colin had put up stage times in many cases better than most of the Scandinavians. A works car was loaned for the rest of the home rallies, and all three Nationals were mopped up, namely, the Bolton, the Vales, and the Castrol Express and Star. With other club rally victories, Malkin/Brown had collected enough points to be untouchable in the MN Championship.

An entry on the RAC was then put aside in favour of riding three up in a works Hunter on the London-to-Sydney of which more anon.

A mixed year of fortune dogged Colin's 1969 rallying activities, although before Rootes pulled out of the game, he did convincingly win the Manx. Then a number of outings followed in a Jolly Club (etc) Lancia Fulvia 1300, though usually terminating in retirement. A brand-new 1.6 HF was used on the RAC, but that too retired.

For 1970, a switch to Ford machinery with Monte practising and World Cup, European and South American recces. All this—as we go to press—in preparation for the greatest rally of all time; the Daily Mirror's World Cup. Colin co-driven, it is hoped, by Richard Hudson-Evans, will be using a 2-litre Escort.

chapter 1

CHOOSING THE CAR

ALTHOUGH it is *possible* to collect major awards on any rally in a car that is generally accepted amongst the devotees of rallying as totally unsuitable—mentioning no names, of course—generally speaking, there are really only a few economically sound propositions currently available on the market.

Obviously any car can be rallied. But with special-stage motoring becoming more and more important, and all those rocks, an enthusiast would do best to follow the herd, and stick to popular marques. This may seem mundane, unexciting and biased, but it'll not only be cheaper —you may even win. It's so important to make the right choice of car to start off with. Rallying *is* expensive, but the right car can save money in the long run.

Currently there are four distinct types of rallying open to British competitors. Starting off at the cheaper, and less serious, end of the scale, there are masses of minor— and sometimes regional championship—events which remain basically navigational, and thankfully devoid of top brass. Secondly, there are the leading club events, usually counting towards the Castrol Motoring News Championship, which are certainly not for beginners. Then there are the Nationals, which seem to become less and less numerous each year, due to insurance and authorisation difficulties, and the home Internationals, such as the Welsh, Scottish, Circuit of Ireland and the RAC. Although some of the Nationals do have selectives, which are basically very tight sections on public roads—although in many cases one couldn't imagine a member of the public taking a family barge along the route—timed to the nearest second and set at an uncleanable 30 m.p.h. average, the top events tend to be special-stage orientated. Finally there is the Continental classic, like the Alpine, which due to devaluation and political instability, has to remain a dream as far as entering is concerned nowadays. The British percentage of the entry at European events seems to have fallen right off, and those who still go—outside the shelter of a works team—are, in the main, nostalgic amateurs, who only do one or two events per annum to give them something to talk about for the rest of their inactive off-season. But whatever your pretensions may be, and wherever your arena of activity finally is, you must get the right car first.

As public, police and parliamentary opinions are basically anti-rallying, that is until we have a few rallying MPs, the end of the traditional road rally is regrettably ultimately on the cards. All the above types of rallying—right down to the smallest closed-to-club rally —include rough stuff, if not in the form of out-and-out special stages or the meat of the road section, as tie-deciding sections, to avoid the embarrassment of too many penalty-free runs. The ability of the car and driver to maintain high averages over rough going on private property is all-important, and, as a useful trainer for the forests, this is now what rallying is all about. So whatever car you choose, it must be suitable for rough work, albeit after some basic preparation.

The choice

Look carefully at any entry list for a major British club event—you will see Cortinas, Escorts, Hunters, Imps and the proverbial Mini variants in predominance. British Leyland Land-Crabs, 1100s, Spridgets or MGBs are used, as are the occasional Vauxhall, Anglia variants, VWs, Volvos Lancias, and any rallyman's ultimate—the Porsche. But follow the basic rules—rally what the works or major tuning firms do. Parts—and more important the right, tested, competition parts should be available. These will be far cheaper than ones for an exotic alternative, and above all, most of the snags will have been discovered already.

This advice is obviously not going to be applicable where minor class wins on obscure Internationals are sought; for this task a Chinese perambulator with a brace of moped engines might prove to be more successful, in terms of pots and bonuses, than a full-house Escort Twin-Cam from Boreham. But in this country, the field of possibles that I would suggest you consider for rally use are all capable of winning a major home event with the right ingredients. The final choice of car must also be influenced by the finance available, and the sort of use outside rallying that the vehicle will be expected to undertake. There is obviously no better way to break up a happy home than to prepare a carpetless "Special Stage Screamer" as your rally wagon if it has to double up as regular transport for Granny to go to the whist drive—that is unless she is deaf or used to go on motorcycle trials in the dark ages. In the same vein, a Cortina, complete with rally gear, is a much better bet for taking kids on an ice-cream hunt than a Group 6 Imp.

Rallying, like all sections of motor sport, is getting more and more specialised, so if you really want to fly with a chance of winning, then you have to keep your rally car exclusively for the noble Saturday night sport of hammering down cart tracks—and no stopping in gateways either. The man who can select his chariot without being influenced by outside ties on the extra-rally use of his car is in the most favourable position, as he then has at least one principal ingredient for success.

So as not to put off the majority of readers who are not in the millionaire set, nor in the motor trade, let me say that surprisingly an out-and-out rally car need not be all that expensive. Naturally one's degree of mechanical prowess, plus what home workshop facilities you have on hand, dictate the total cost to a large extent. But a built-up Min to 1300 "S" spec, a secondhand Imp, revamped to works-modded 998 trim, or a Mk. 1 Cortina, with all the acknowledged alterations, can be prepared for between £300 and £500. I know of several examples from this price range which have won major Welsh thrashes. Lotus-Cortinas, Mk. 2s, and Twin-Cam Escorts tend to cost very much more.

Buying secondhand

For those that don't want to build from scratch there's always a ready-prepared rally car that is someone else's throw-out. This isn't all that foolish, for at least everything will have been done, and in most cases it'll only be a thorough overhaul of basic assemblies that will be necessary, without having to go out and buy all the special parts, before you can start off rallying. All the rally gear is usually left intact on an old rally car, and depending on who the previous owner is and when he last used the car in action, it could be all set for the next event. You can select such a car from the classified columns of the enthusiast press. But don't always be put off by ripples or crunch evidence. Although such scars will naturally affect the resale value of the car, the sound-ness of the mechanical vitals, and the standard of preparation, are the most important.

Mini, Imp, Cortina or Escort—the field is narrowed down, and they're all entirely different to drive. On the rougher events, the Mini is bound to receive the worst punish-ment underneath. A Mini has two big disadvantages, small wheels and a low ground clearance. It probably handles best, for the novice anyway, and is certainly the most forgiving. Initially, it's the cheapest to prepare, although the replacement cost of so many components at frequent inter-vals makes you the best of friends with your local BMC dealer. Apart from virtually every tuning firm selling modifications for the Mini the centre of the bolt-on bazaar is BMC Special Tuning at Abingdon. All the bits that have been used in anger with success are listed in their sheets, and can be ordered through the usual channels.

Imps are the least used by private owners at the moment—but perhaps with their rallycross potential being demonstrated occasionally on the box most weekends, I feel sure that this position may shortly change. Many of the lessons learnt from the Imp's rally successes have been passed on to the private owner by the now defunct Rootes Com-petitions, in the same way as Special Tuning and the Ford Per-formance Centre champion the Mini and Ford causes respectively. Imps have large wheels and healthy ground clearances, with the power unit and transaxle at the rear of the car as an aid to maximum traction. Even on the roughest events, like the Scottish, the Imp has proved in its 998 form to be a contender for outright victory, whilst on the snow and ice of a Monte, a class success could be an annual affair. Currently there are not that many firms in-volved in Imp tuning and rally preparation, many still clinging to the Mini and Ford bandwagon. But with the 1968 example of home championships in the Rootes bag, perhaps private owners will be using them before long.

Fords are the most expensive of the selected trio to set up, but they seem to stay in trim longest. Easily the best double-up car for ordinary road use, the Ford manages to accommodate extra bods and luggage even with long range tanks and spare wheels in the boot. But a Cortina is a big car, and when pressing on it takes up a whole lot of road, which makes it a difficult car to get the maximum out of to begin with. It also suffers from the handicap of having its driven wheels at the opposite end to engine and box. On the other hand, a well-built Cortina is by far the strongest for the truly diabolical offerings of some Northern rally organisers' routes. And the Escort, whether Twin-Cam or big pushrod, is undoubtedly "in" too.

So the final decision is all a matter of marque allegiance, and what drive/engine configurations **you** prefer.

The lower your chariot, the more this sort of servicing may become necessary. Hopkirk's Mini on the Acropolis.

You can rally anything!

Colin Malkin and Keith Wood sliding the Jolly Club Lancia during the '69 RAC Rally.

Colin Malkin is—would you believe —awake!

chapter 2

UNDERBODY PROTECTION

INSTANT cart track motoring—under any weather conditions—can be obtained by purchasing a well known Russian vehicle that can absorb the very worst that the Steppes can produce, or go out and buy that well known product of Stuttgart. But both these extremes may be above, or beyond, your political or financial leanings. With the right sorting it's quite amazing what unlikely contraption can win an event. But it's all done the hard way—in the private owner's garage, which is far away from all the glamorous action.

But whatever the car, the very mildest introduction to nocturnal bog trotting or forestry scenic tours will rather rapidly instil on every participant the number one priority of underbody protection.

It's a very great advantage in rallying to have the underside of your car prepared like a tank's. This is all the more essential if premature retirement is to be avoided. Far too many people rush out to load the front of their cars with a galaxy of lights, or cram as many carbs as possible onto their motors; showing more concern in satisfying the whims of their local goody supplier or engine tuner than using plain common sense. Underbody protective devices are the very first consideration, and are far and away the most important of all the other paraphernalia. So look to your chariot's vulnerable under regions before you expend too much thought and cash on worrying about improvements to go, stop, ride, night visual aids or crew comfort. What is more important to most genuine privateers is that with an intact underside you might even be able to drive your car to and from work in the following week, as well as home after the event.

Whatever car you eventually decide upon—or are forced to use by the usual dreaded financial crisis, is all part and parcel of every enthusiast's choice of what they can use and what events they are able to do in their steed, don't forget to skid every protrusion underneath so that the underside is as smooth as possible. It isn't all that expensive—even if you have to get someone to do it for you and keep him and all his mates in grog for a few minutes. Obviously this may seem a little too much as "what the works do," for the one or two-events-a-year type. But even if a fairly localised season is planned, it'll really pay off in terms of protecting your investment, as well as giving you some peace of mind when cannoning across the rough at a race track—or even the local's car park! One thing is absolutely certain, money spent on the underside isn't wasted anywhere.

The higher the better

The lower the car, the more important it is to realise that the bottom will be called upon at most events to act as a very noisy fifth wheel. Even on the highest ground clearance of a Rover 3 Litre and the like, there are occasions when all the wheels will tuck up into the wheel arches and a rally car has to stand up to monocycling on its floor pan. Anyone who has marshalled or spectated on a stage will realise what a pounding even a tail ender's car gets underneath, often the noise of rocks cascading about underneath is far louder than the rortiest exhaust.

If you hope to compete in and complete a very heavy programme of rallies in the same car, and hope to avoid having to pension off the bodyshell too frequently, it is best to strip out all the mechanical assemblies and trim prior to the grand weld and braze. If you've got welding gear, or access to it, all well and good; otherwise as long as you can strip the shell out yourself and deliver same, it shouldn't cost too much to bribe your tame welder, blacksmith or body repairer into stitching up the shell and frames properly. Every motor manufacturer

these days is guilty of leaving undone those things that they ought to have done, and doing those things which they ought not to have done! They are all forced to build to a price for Mr. Everyman who isn't supposed to go off on rallies at the weekends. The odd blob of spot weld every six inches or so just won't do for a really heavy season. All attachment points, such as where shock absorbers are spigot-attached to body panels, or where springs or struts butt against flimsy box sectioning, should be beefed up with plates. These should be welded in place not only to spread the load resulting from enthusiastic yump-ings but also to lengthen the life span of the mass produced tin can that passes as a bodyshell. With models that are rallied regularly by the circus, the reinforcement places can easily be discovered from con-sultation with the works competition departments, their satellite tuning concerns, or leading private owners, who in many cases are proprietors of enthusiast garages.

The ravages of the traditional grassy hummocks can be kept at bay by the judicious application of sundry scraps of sheet metal, tack welded onto all protrusions in the form of skids. Edges of valences and silencer boxes should be shielded by making up mini-guards. The bottoms of silencers and their edges should be plated both as a skid and also as a reinforcement against eventual squashing. At this juncture it goes without saying (too much anyway) that silencers should be mounted as high as possible to get them right up out of the way. As an example of the ultimate I'll quote my old works prepared Imp on which the silencer was safely out of the way and did—despite the occasional spin terminating in cessation of backwards motion against the stoutest bank—remain sound absorbing and intact, even after many events.

Silencers

Silencers, regardless of the shelter offered to them by their location, should be securely affixed. The mounting rubbers should be duplicated and preferably of a tougher, and harder, grade. Quite often, a larger model in a manufacturer's range fits just the right mounting for the rallying owner of a smaller model, or the shelves of your local motor factor are bound to have something suitable. The duplication of mountings so that there is a spare set all ready mounted alongside the standard ones is very important to aid speedy attachment of a new system or re-attachment of the old one if you've gone and knocked it off while going off the road in the middle of an event. At least this way, the delay whilst servicing the exhaust will be kept to the absolute minimum. Remember the future of rallying is always in jeopardy every time a rally car thrashes on with its exhaust smashed away.

Straight through systems

Every serious campaigner has been guilty in his or her time of trying to finish a rally with a straight-through system—sans silencer. But if we all face up to it this sort of thing has to be a thing of the past, even if there was nothing like the racket of a few ex-works Healeys rocketing down the Elan valley with what amounted to full race, and pre-decibel-conscious exhausts. A badly blown exhaust must spell instant retirement in modern GB night rallying rules; so make sure yours stays together by building it up properly in the first place.

Still on the exhausts remember that even with the aces at the navigational helm, you do have to make the occasional rapid reverse down the most diabolical going imaginable—so tack your skids onto the system on both sides. There's no earthly use in making a man-size job of the leading edge of a silencer box for 100 m.p.h. plus on the rough, if at the first 5 m.p.h. reverse by our "ace pilote" the unit rips open on a thistle causing instant retirement. It never ceases to amaze me how many Cortinas go rallying—after some very expensive preparation bills from the acknowledged experts—with their rear lower bodywork torn back and distorted by contact with the rough.

The most expensive and involved conversion to the underside of a rally car, which is likely to tax even the most ingenious, and which one or two Marathon cars dabbled with, is to build a special compartment above floor level on one side of the shell to accommodate the pipes. This boxed in master-canal has to encroach on the navigator's side of things and can even, as on the last of the works rally Healey 3000s, absorb the exhaust system. Naturally, if someone has to sit above this newly introduced box section for very long, it's wise to insulate the tunnel, so that it's heat and flame proof. On the Healey, the passenger's door had been shortened, and the navigator's seat was more inclined than the driver's. In this way, the problem of keeping a system intact, plus the pipework too, had been solved.

Sideways motoring

Guard against the results of sideways motoring too; watch sills, jacking points and drain plugs. Hydraulic brake hoses should be sheathed with coil springs, but not so their movement is impeded or you may get a fracture at the union. Apart from the safety benefit to be derived from having armoured brake hoses, it certainly helps one to boot it at a decent rate of knots down a rocky descent with the confidence that at the point of anchoring up you will at least have a pedal. If a complete build from scratch programme is on the cards then a very good idea is to build up a new set of bundy tubing. Before fitting the olives and swaging over the tubing, sheath the bundy with lengths of clear PVC fuel tubing. This way, the possibilities of a fast moving flint zinging through a brake pipe will be avoided, and the hydraulic system will also be guaranteed a long and safe life. Another point, with all this attention to the brake pipes and hoses, is that if an off-the-road excursion takes place and the car should be severely distorted, then at least the fluidics will still stand a chance of functioning.

If at all possible within the class regulations and the RAC's vehicle regs, move anything from underneath that is vulnerable. Petrol tanks can so easily be raised. Batteries can be moved and fuel pumps repositioned. But if it's impossible or impractical to move underbody units, then guard them well.

The attachment and fabrication of suitable guards is not all that complicated and is certainly not beyond the capabilities of even the most basic do-it-yourselfer. But please beware of the instant brightly painted solution to underbody protection. Bright paint isn't necessarily the answer to the slot basher's dream—and there really is a great deal of bilge being marketed by the purveyors of instant success. Battery, petrol tanks, fuel pumps, gearbox and differential guards are a must—but when all's said and done, they are only bits of metal, albeit painted, bent and labelled attractively. If you do buy instant units, don't be done by wasting your money on pretty mods, for you'll only leave yourself with less money to get on with the action. So, buy from reputable suppliers and, only go for replica guards, that are at least being used by the better and more successful clubmen.

Rubber buffers

Another point to follow when fitting guards to a rally car is to install rubber padding between the guard and the vital component. This way you will avoid the disconcerting drumming and rattling, when half way through an event the guards have been hammered up by all the rocks and both crewmen spend a great deal of valuable road time trying to fathom out what is (or is about to become) adrift. Do watch out that the rubber is kept well away from the really hot points such as the base of the exhaust manifold, for it could be a most embarrassing source of fire. If you can get hold of the sort of rubber that is used to mount heavy presses and factory machinery, this seems to be smoulder proof and fills in the air gap between the sump and guard very effectively. Another advantage for the rubber is that it cuts out the chance of a stone becoming lodged between the guard and the sump, which can at a later time— usually in the middle of the longest special stage of a rally—get pushed through the sump when the guard gets a mighty wallop.

When preparing a used car for rallies; it's wise to fit a new set of lines inside the shell—this covers the battery cable, the brake pipes, as well as the fuel pipe. Ideally, these should be fitted to the sides of the shell where it's double skinned and right up out of the way from a side or underbody graunch. Route the lines so that they are well clear of stray feet and seat mechanisms. Always grommet the lines where they pass through panels and protect them from navigators, who seem bent on destroying everything around the footwell of their side of the car which must confirm that all navigators are frustrated drivers at heart!

There are certain cases where it isn't at all practical to move the lines inside the shell so they have to be shielded in situ. Use strips of rubber and conduit—preferably tack welding the steel strip or conduit to the shell. Screws and bolts never seem to be very satisfactory underneath the body; over a big rally mileage they tend to rattle free. This sort of cover-up preparation has worked surprisingly well on quite a few private owners' Cooper 998s, 850s and Ss where it's been too difficult to move the hydrolastic pipework inside.

Fasteners

When securing cable and pipe eyelets to floor pans, use pop rivets in preference to self-tapping screws. Self-tappers are nice and easy, but they tend to catch on grassy hummocks, which does the floor no good at all. They are also rather painful if you rasp against their ends when doing some work underneath. By the time you've secured

A silencer box, skidded front and back for both ways motoring.

all the lines and pipes to the floor pan adequately, if you use self-tappers it'll begin to resemble a porcupine's back.

Fasteners can be neatly and simply fabricated from a sheet of aluminium. A strip the size of the clip required, should be scribed out on the aluminium, and then cut out using a pair of tin snips. Wrapping this round the cable or pipe to be secured, helps to form the correct shape. After drilling the right size of hole through the body and the clip, the clip can be secured by a rivet. If the pipe ever needs removing for servicing, it should be secured by a self-tapping screw. It's also a good idea to bind the cable or pipe in question before inserting it in the clip, in order to prevent possible chaffing.

The ultimate here would be a full-length undershield, but this would be very heavy unless made from hardened dural and in any case would be very expensive.

Don't have any guard securing bolts fitted with their threads downwards as the bolts will only bend and the threads become so jagged that they won't release the nuts without a chisel and a struggle. Try if possible to weld bolt heads to the guards, so that they're captive. If you have to have the bolts fitted with their threads downwards, due to the fact that if they were captive the other way up you wouldn't be able to get a spanner into the space available to tighten up the nuts, then countersink a platform into the guard for them. This way, the nuts are less likely to get damaged and can easily be undone with a box spanner, leaving the bolts welded in place, all set to slot the guard back onto the car with the minimum time loss. It's as well to remember, when reinforcing the body shell and various vital sections of subframes, that the stronger the sump or underbody guard, the more likelihood there is of whatever the guard is attached to folding up as the next weak link.

chapter 3

SETTING UP THE CAR

ONE of the most obvious characteristics that every rallyist must build into his chariot is that of as near perfect handling and stopping as is possible—but always with reliability in mind. So sacrifices have to be quite often made against the ultimate in goodies. The real skill in "setting up" a rally car is surely in the conductor's results in the money —without the instant negative camber kit falling apart, or the experimental plasticine suspension units disintegrating half way through an event!

It's sad to think that cost has to come into the choice of suspension bits and brake mods. But there are very few cars that can safely be taken straight from the showroom and pounded round even the mildest club rally without all sorts of ex-sales handout horrors looming up—like aerated dampers, odd clunks from all four corners, or, worst of all, a brake pedal that decides to go to the floor on the very first tight section. But, place "setting up" components as a second priority on your budget's list, after underbody protection. All the power in the world,

the best navigator's slot reading, and the most skilful driving is completely wasted if your rally car doesn't go roughly in the desired direction—not only instantly, but all the time. Most cars can be sorted, so that their handling and stopping is vice-free. If you choose to be a pioneer with a previously unrallied machine, then you'll just have to proceed in this aspect of preparation by trial and error. But if the regulars have already used, or better still, are currently still campaigning a replica of your own car—then you would save yourself a great deal of unnecessary experimenting in this direction by assiduously copying their specifications.

Unfortunately, different tuning firms have quite often entirely different ideas on how a particular model should be set up. For those who are fortunate enough to have chosen a car that is currently being rallied by a motor manufacturer— then the part numbers and know-how required can usually be obtained from their tuning sheets or parts counters (Ford's Performance Centre at Boreham through FoMoCo dealers, or British Leyland Special Tuning through BMC parts division). But, even with the factories reckoning on what should be used, several leading private exponents beg to differ, which all helps to make the whole business of what should or should not be altered, so much more interesting.

Compromise

Suffice it to say in setting up, a compromise has to be struck, so that the ride height is acceptable for the sort of terrain that one has to traverse, and that the spring rates, plus the degree of damping, has to be tuned to the amount of weight that is being propelled over the rally route. Quite obviously there must be a sacrifice in the ultimate handling if the ground clearance has to be upped, with stiffer dampers fitted. In fact the theoretical maximum cornering speed will naturally be reduced. But, whatever freakish handling you introduce by mods to your suspension, ensure that the car still handles in a controllable fashion. Fore and aft pitching is not only very retrogressive towards a crew being able to keep the whole deal on the road—it's dangerous and wastes time. The fastest way home is between the hedges!

In the same vein, there is no earthly use in having such powerful dampers that the shockers get punched through the panels on the rough stuff, or their mountings get bent double on the first culvert. Ensure that the dampers that you select are not too firm and above all that they absorb shock, rather than double up as bump stops or full travel restrictors. So many folks assume that wishy-washy handling is immediately cured by bolting on "go-go" dampers. The springs must

be the right rate for the weight carried, taking into account the sort of going the long suffering machinery is going to be expected to conquer.

Another point to watch on "setting up" is to keep it simple. The less gear there is, the less there is to give trouble, and the cheaper it is to go round replacing components periodically. Dampers, suspension joints and springs do deteriorate; like every working part on a rally car, they must be changed regularly.

Tyres and wheels

Coupled with stiffening up the suspension and raising the height where necessary, it's also very important to select the right tyres and wheels. The tyres should be selected according to the event; in general for UK rallying as it is at the moment radial knobblies are "in". If there is going to be a series of tarmac selectives or speed hill climbs, then it goes without saying that a serious exponent will use racing tyres on a spare set of wheels. But, until you are ready to win and can afford buying shares in a tyre factory, this is rather a waste. Balance weights never seem to stay on wheels for very long on a rally, so you'll be doing most of your motoring with the discomfort of wobbly wheels. It's one of the many little inconveniences you'll have to get used to—like going to work on the bus after every event! Your wheel rims will very quickly look like threepenny bits. Fit tubes—De Luxe or Racing if possible—and get used to hurling tyres onto the scrap tip every time a bubble appears in the wall. It may seem a waste to throw tyres away that still have plenty of tread left on them, but it just isn't worth risking a blowout. Look for tread cuts and bulges on the inside walls. Apart from the danger, punctures cost time on a competitive section.

The choice of brand is all a matter of personal preference. Don't dismiss remoulds either as some of them—particularly Kentreads and Motorway Remoulds—are fine even for the most arduous and rocky motoring. My advice though is to use tyres that are readily available from most tyre dealers, so that replacements are at least a possibility. If you are going on the larger events, use the same make and type as the works cars. In any case, use tyres that will mean that you'll be eligible for any support from the friendly tyre trucks of that very well known manufacturer who spends so much on our section of the sport (no commercials of course . . .).

Too many folk go mad with over-wide wheels. Forget what the wheels look like. After all, once they're muddy, you cannot see pretty colours, or recognise flashy motifs anyway! Although the Healeys used wire wheels for season after season, they tend to be very expensive to keep in true. Alloy wheels often seem to chip or shed lumps if forestry stages are attacked with any sideways vigour. But magnesium alloy wheels are a different matter. Not only are they very light—but they get plenty of cooling air to the brakes, and are immensely strong. I've even seen cars finish stages on a Minilite rim after the tyre has burst and been worn away. What has staggered me is that on occasions like these the wheels are often salvageable. The only snag for many private owners is that they are rather costly— especially when it means making a complete change to this type of

wheel, and this can involve several sets of wheels. Otherwise, it's wide steel wheels, a hammer handy to keep the rims in shape, and a careful periodic look at the centres, to ensure that they aren't breaking up.

Don't overdo widening, it's quite unnecessary for road/stage rallying. With too much non-slip rubber on the road, you'll put extra strain on your overworked transmission as well as wheel bearings. Often you'll tend to experience graunching in the wheel arches on humps, or when the suspension has sagged.

Another legal point to watch, when you push a whole lot of rubber out of the wheel arches because of a really wide set of wheels, is that this tyre tread area is capped with protective spats, which are very vulnerable on any rally car that is going to be enterprisingly driven. Spats catch on log piles and "lean-to" banks. They also get squashed when you have to tip the car on its side to glue the underside together again half way through a rally!

Brakes

Brakes are very much a part of "setting up" any rally wagon. At the very least you should change over to competition brake pads and/or linings. Although far too many British drivers use their brakes far too much, you must still ensure that they are as fade free as is possible. Currently Ferodo are the world leaders in the competition brake material field—and virtually every machine is catered for admirably by their gargantuan stock.

Servos are fitted to many sporting cars as standard, though in many cases drivers prefer not to have them connected as they tend to lock the wheels up too easily, as well as losing much of the feel that is so important when delicate pedal work is called for. On the other hand, a servo is very good as an anti-fatigue mod, and for those with weak ankles they at least produce sufficient pedal pressure at the braking material to retard forward motion.

Most cars these days have vastly improved brakes fitted as standard, which makes quite a change from some of the cars that used to rocket down the Welsh mountains ten years ago. Perhaps, the only reason that they were able to put up such alarmingly rapid times, was that their brakes had melted away several hundred feet back up the mountain and their brake pedals were therefore merely being used for somewhere to rest their feet! Anyway that's where the manufacturers learnt their lessons! Because of the average braking systems on popular cars these days, it's quite often only a matter of changing over to competition linings and you're all set for the rally. But still, older models can so very easily be converted by tacking on the latest stoppers. For instance, 850 Minis can be transformed to the rapidity of downhill travel in safety, by changing a set of single wheel cylinder front anchors to the later twin leading shoe variety, or better still to S calipers, discs and shafts.

chapter 4

SETTING UP EXAMPLES

THERE are all manner of trade tricks to copy when preparing a rally car in the suspension, brake, wheel and tyre departments; the necessary improvements vary from one model to the other and from one rallyist to the other. Even those without one of the listed models below will be able to find many of the points covered of use to them as a general guide. The more different makes the better as it all makes the current rally scene so much more interesting; not just for the manufacturers and the crews—but for the spectators.

The following sample cars are all popularly campaigned with a fair amount of success. Obviously opinions on how to set up each of these cars—or indeed variants of them—vary immensely. So to give ample food for thought. If your own favourite marque has been omitted try to note only what can be appropriated to your own particular model. It would take an enormous time to deal with every one.

Dry suspension Minis

Warwickshire's David Hirons has prepared many dry suspension Minis for club rallying so he's used to building Minis that stay together. Before attempting serious stage events he advises having both subframes welded up in the prescribed places. He fits stronger tie bars than even the latest S ones at the front. These are so thick that they would probably be the last parts to bend in a shunt! He fits the latest type lower arms with strengthened bracing joints which consist of further bars welded between the tie bars and the lower arms. A touch of the racer look is applied with 1½ degrees negative at the front. With the brake hoses being so vulnerable on the Mini. Dave only fits the competition brake hoses, identifiable by two green bands and protective plastic coil springing. Even if a servo is used by a customer he likes to see all his customers rally away with S brakes all round assuming, that is, they're not competing in an 850 Group 2 car. You have to have Ferodo DS 11s at the front with VG 95s at the rear. Although not strictly connected with "setting up", it's as well to cover all the brake piping with plastic fuel tubing where it runs outside the body shell even on the run across the front of the frame before final fitting into position and swaging. As Mini lower arm pins have been known to come adrift on a stage, these should be fitted with drilled castellated nuts and split pins. Just the right amount of damping at the front is provided by fitting a pair of Armstrong shockers at race settings, but these should ideally be loosened by a period of normal motoring or running-in prior to being used in action. Naturally the shocker bushes should be flanked with sturdy washers which will at least keep most of the bushes in place until you're home again. Flat washers and spring washers should also be used on the front shocker top mounting plates where they are attached to the body, as they have a tendency of coming adrift after a little pattering. At the back of dry Minis Dave reckons that you ought to fix up one degree of negative at the suspension pivot pin outer mounting plates. The rear frame should be welded up so that both lower runs are coated with skid plates or else they tend to buckle and progressively wear away on the rough stuff. The exhaust mountings ought to be beefed up also, so that, with double rubbers in the centre channel, there is no chance of the exhaust coming adrift. Both rear arms must have skids attached to them to protect the brake bundy piping as well as the wheel cylinder nipples. This welded plate should run from the rear suspension arms to the backplate bottoms. Ideally, the wheel cylinders should have their pins removed prior to drilling of the cylinder body and backplate. Then this should be tapped to take a 2 BA screw. This

avoids the usual Mini rear end curse of the wheel cylinders twisting on their circlips. Van rear struts—the cast aluminium ones—should be slotted in. These can of course be shortened to drivers' requirements; if the car is too low, packing washers can be inserted. Armstrong shockers, set at their softest, are fitted at the rear. It's also very important to fit taper roller rear wheel bearings, as they do at least last. Another important point to watch is that the rear shocker top mounting holes through the shell are in good condition. These tend to take a great deal of punishment and ought to be reinforced by plenty of welding as, after a great deal of roughery, the spot welded hole plates tend to become detached from the rest of the shell. It has even been known for the wheel arches to pull away from the main shell. So braze up the shell along all the seams before you start rallying and don't have your shockers too hard as it won't do the body any good at all.

Fit all rally Minis with 4½ to 5½ rims all round—and don't over-rim as you'll only put more strain than is built into the design onto the suspension, wheel bearings, hubs and transmission. The wider you go with wheels, the wider spacers you need; it all means that you'll have more to catch on the sides of the route.

Hydrolastic Minis

Will Sparrow, Cars and Car Conversions Team member, is undoubtedly the Midland's No. 1 Mini Man at the moment. He has prepared many Minis for all sorts of destructive uses, and so his advice on "setting up" a wet one is very worthwhile heeding. Will always kits Minis with the latest S displacers, namely double blue units. These should be linked with internal flexible piping. Ideally all four corners ought to be fitted with individual taps in the lines so that each corner can be isolated in the event of a failure somewhere along the fluidic line.

Wet Minis can be left standard at the back—although the Special Tuning competition helper springs are very good. These are the ones identifiable with orange bands. With a set of large Aeon bump rubbers plus these tougher springs the back is kept in check and the evil see-sawing effect of the hydrolastic suspension is eliminated. Will also inserts a tenth of an inch thick spacer between the cone and the top arm ball joint. Finally the pressure of both sides of the system is pushed above the official limit to 300—but this depends on a driver's personal preference.

All Sparrow's Minis have been kitted out with Ferodo DS 11 pads/ VG 95 linings with or without servo ; although it is interesting to note that Will always uses a servo on his own "S". He also uses the standard "S" pressure limiting valve. Will emphasises the need for gas welding all the sub-frame seams and in particular the tie bar mountings before you go in for the tougher events. The back frame needs adequately skidding, or else not only will the suspension not stay set up for very long, but you'll stand quite a good chance of pulling the frame out of the shell. Extra front shocker kits are a good plan and effectively damp those cars that develop yo-yo tendencies.

British Leyland 1100s and 1300s

Basil Wales of British Leyland Special Tuning, Abingdon, Berkshire, knows exactly what needs to be done to all BL models. Apart from the occasional Rallycross, BL has really hardly used the 1100/1300 for any hard rally motoring so there's very little catalogued. There are few special bits and pieces—and what is rather surprising is that you don't need to do much. The displacers off the Cooper S are not interchangeable, and the standard units are apparently quite up to Marathons on the one hand, and club events on the other. So, the private owner has little to do. A set of Aeon bump rubbers at the back is about it.

One thing is very important, don't run the hydrolastic suspension pressure under the 205 lb. sq. in. mark unless you enjoy inducing car sickness to your back seat drivers. The 210 lb. setting for the system is just about right. It's also a complete waste of time trying to fix up some negative camber on the 1100. It might look racey, but there are apparently no advantages in A to B times as a result. With Mk. 1 brakes, you ought to change over to the C-AHT 16 conversion set at the front, and on the Mk. 2 and the BL 1300 GTs you already have progressive braking as standard. The servo through BMC—or rather British Leyland/Cowley/Austin/Morris Parts Division—under their part number 8G-8732 is a good mod for any 1100. Even with competition pads at the front, standard brake linings are best at the back, as at least a decently effective handbrake will still be possible. If the rear end tends to lock up at the slightest hint of a provocation on the driver's part, then the pressure limiting valve will need doctoring by changing to a less sensitive one, or for those who enjoy being Mini-Butchers, get the file at the limiting valve's spring and grind a bit off. If a Group 5 or 6 category is to be entered, and a dual braking system is required, then Special Tuning do a dual brake master cylinder C-AJJ 338, which incidentally fits Minis as well. This costs about £8 and comes complete with the necessary piping to split the front and back brakes hydraulically. The master cylinder reservoir is larger too, and the level is immediately visible through the transparent body. If you order one of these kits, you must state whether your motor is right or left-hand drive as the bundy is a different length run.

The pipework for the hydrolastic is fairly well protected in the tunnel, so, if only grassy ventures are to be undertaken, there's little point in going to town on putting everything inside. One Special Tuning part, that is worth tacking on, is their petrol tank shield which is made out of thick glassfibre and can be ordered like all the rest of the goodies through an Austin/Morris dealer under part number C-AJT176.

The British Leyland 1800

The specification of 1800s has varied quite a lot since they were first introduced and although basically they may appear the same to the casual glance, many mods have been carried out gradually on the production line as a direct result of the East African Safari, Marathon and Southern Cross entries. One of the leading tuning firms, which prepares 1800s for all sorts of rallying, is undoubtedly Janspeed Engineering Ltd., Southampton Road, Salisbury, Wiltshire. The setting up interpretation of Jan Odor is therefore of great value to all Land-Crab—or rather Jan-Crab proprietors. BL Special Tuning of course list plenty of parts for this well developed machine.

The Mk. 2 1800 is pretty good in standard trim for club events anyway, but if any 1800 is beset with the dreaded pitching on a humpy road, then it needs a rear anti-roll bar with standard displacers all independently piped. This means that all four corners are truly independent of each other and there are no linking fluidics. This way, a car can be set up as required, with individual settings or pressures as required, with any bias on hand, merely by adjusting the pressure at the individual corner or end. This system also does away with the interconnecting pipework and so there's no need to go in for all the elaborate taps and internal hydrolastic pipework that are so expensive to install. If this may seem a little too serious for 1800 owners with only ordinary rallying in mind, then the standard set up is alright with the following mods: Armstrong or Konis on the rear, keep or fit the rear anti-roll bar, fit Aeon bump rubbers, and fit all the pipes and lines inside or shield them very thoroughly.

It was interesting to note that on the Marathon the many Janspeed prepared 1800s used front 1800 displacers at the back, because of the colossal load of spares and equipment that were on board. Jan also fitted all the 1800s with bump and rebound stops.

There will be a competition displacer available sometime for the 1800 owner, but at the time of going to press this is still not available.

The height of an 1800 is variable by altering two things—the wheel diameter and the hydrolastic pressure. Janspeed reckon that 1800s motor best on 14″ wheels of the magnesium variety with a 4.1 axle ratio. For those that cannot run to mags, then 13″ x 5½ Js steel are all right. With the larger wheels, and the suspension blown up to 250 lbs. the average all-up weight of a Janspeed Marathon 1800 car was 32/33 cwt.—and with these mods, they still seemed to handle well!

One thing that Jan is very keen on is safety. So for any 1800 owner who wants to jump about the woods you must have a dual braking kit. Jan does twin master cylinders, plus a balance bar and all the fittings for £50. And, whether a servo is fitted or not, and whether the car has dual braking or not—Janspeed again advise all privateers to use Ferodo pads and linings, namely DS11s at the front and VG95s at the back.

Well, that just about rounds up BL setting up. If owners of sportscars feel that they've been left out of it, then I'll just have to say that virtually every sportscar—except the Porsche —is hardly suitable as a rallyable proposition these days: they just don't have the ground clearance. Some of you will cry out well what about the Nova MGB and John Sprinzel's Midget—they were even put in for the Marathon! And then John has used an MGC on the last Monte too. Well, the Nova B looked very nice and "fab gear" with all its trimmings and that's about it . . . whilst John Sprinzel does after all sell MGs, so it's a little different, and sensible, judging by the number of happy octagonal sportscar fans that take delivery of shiny Lancaster Mews sporting carriages. The nostalgic may even throw the Grand Daddy of the alps at me—the Healey 3000. They were great—yes. But they quite honestly belong in the motor sporting history books nowadays, along with the legendary Sunbeam Rapier, XK 120s, and the

Talbot 90 before that.

Imps

Who better to ask what needs to be done than Des O'Dell—Rootes Competition and Customer Tuning Manager.

Any Imp that's going to be used on the rough needs a set of RAC springs. These stiffen the Imp up and also raise it nice and clear of the rocks. The part numbers are CTS/7103427 for the front and CTS/7103020 for the back. At this point, it's as well to ensure that you have the toughest possible undershield at the back. The shield should preferably be the works pattern, as, although it's mighty heavy at 45 lbs., it protects the vital regions of the transaxle from tail banging; Des cannot emphasise enough here that Imp owners should not skimp on their sump guarding. Hard rubber should be fitted—about ½″ thick and 9″ square—between the transaxle and the guard, and soft rubber between the engine and the shield. Initially, wire mesh was scroughed to fill up the gap between the guard and the motor. But lately, this has been superseded at the factory by the rubber sandwich filling. The idea of the padding is to stop stones getting in between the guard and the casings, because on a really savage landing, a stone has been known to be pushed smartly through the ally like a die—even though the guard had retained its original shape, albeit a little higher. The shockers are very important too for cutting out any yo-yo from the new springs. So it must be Armstrong AT 9s at the front (CTS/7103428) which have 8 clicks of adjustment. Four clicks up from their ex-factory out-of-the-box state is a good starting point. At the back, the shockers are different for each side. So order CTS/ 7103422 on the right-hand corner and CTS/7103423 for the left. On the rear you can click away 22 times if you get really desperate, but 10 clicks from maximum should be right. However, the final rear settings can be varied according to a driver's taste. If you find that you've got a wee bit too much oversteer, then stiffen up the AT 9s at the back a few clicks. If you've too much understeer, try to set the car up in a slide before the corner or soften the back. Try to adjust the end of the car the furthest from the end that is playing up. Because this way, you'll still have some adjustment left for counteracting wear during a long event or between the smaller rallies. Naturally, the tyre pressures come into this too. but here you ought to abide by the manufacturers' competition approved setting.

If you've the very early Imp then you must of course eliminate the positive camber at the front for rallying. Most tuning firms who do work on Imps produce a negative camber kit to put the wheels upright. Many of the later cars have low pivot points, so owners of these needn't bother. Unless a very long programme of events is to be undertaken, you needn't weld up seams and the like on the Imp. The bodies are very strong, and even after hundreds of laps round Bagshot they stay firmly stitched together.

Although many Imp owners seem to experiment with weird discery off all sorts of cars the drum brakes on the Imp are really perfectly all right— once they're fitted with VG 95 linings from Ferodo all round. A servo is also a good investment, and here use a Girling Powerstop. If you do have a servo the best master cylinder to use is the .7" one which

means that you will be getting 1½ to 1 effort. On the other hand, if you don't have a servo then try a ⅝" one, as this gives a tolerably light pedal on VGs. Servos are mainly a matter of driver preference, but, at the factory, all the Imps used to have servos, so they have to be right.

The rear links should be changed for the export type which are standard equipment on the Sport or Van. As for the wheels, you cannot do a great deal better than stick to the standard 4½J Imp wheel that originally appeared on the Chamois. These are right for as much power as is feasible on a Clubman's rally car and are quite strong enough, in that the centres don't pull out or the rims become like threepenny bits too rapidly. The factory uses larger wheel nuts which seems to have stemmed from their Rapier days. As is the case with most club rallyists, every Imp is best set up on radial knobblies—and the Rootes team used to swear by Dunlop. Therefore SP 44's it has to be, tubed of course.

Even if you can afford to go on to mags, then you really have no need to go any wider than 4½. I ran on 5" Minilite on the '68 Scottish, but they tended to lead me into a few punctures just when I could have done without them.

One good tip to note when preparing an Imp for a rally is to stop rocks getting down the tunnel in which the gearchange normally resides. This is simply done by making up a shield to go into the tunnel opening so that it's a skidded leading edge. All the lines should be run in this tunnel, although on my Imp the petrol line used to go through the shell where the harness goes. Use a basket affair also under the radiator as has been found necessary under export conditions. This successfully stops stones and projectiles taking the fanbelt off. You also ought to have a fanguard over the fan to try to preserve its blades from stray ball-bearing pebbles.

Anglias

Many clubmen still use the Anglia as their rally car choice. Most of those being used nowadays have followed the Elford example of putting a large motor into the Anglia shell. Undoubtedly, however, the most successful of Anglia exponents was Ron Charlton who used a Perdal prepared example. Peter Dalkin at Perdal is, therefore, very clued up on setting up Anglias—as he is incidentally on far more modern and exotic machinery as well; his customers ranging from Jack Tordoff to a race motor or two for Graham Birrell. Even today, hybrid Anglias, like John Parsons' car are still very competitive.

As most Anglia entrants are very keen types, Perdal find that they are willing to start off with a bare shell, so gas welding presents no problem. All the seams are gone over, and in particular fire and goo is applied to the inner wheelarches. The best thing for the front suspenders is to use Ford Classic heavy-duty struts with Armstrong Roadholder shockers as well. Cortina GT front brakes are a must, as are a set of very heavy springs of 350 lb. rating. Use Classic steering arms, but with different centres so that the steering ratio is as Perdal want it. The body unit at this stage ought to be modified to take the 100E steering box as this transforms the steering apparently. The camber at the front is altered by moving the track control arm centres. With all this little lot at the front, Perdal

manage to obtain 2″ increase in ride height at the front, whereas they reckon to drop the rear 1″. The resultant handling is very good on the loose.

At the back, Perdal put in a second main leaf to wrap round the front eye on each spring set; they then set the springs flatter. For shocks, they favour Armstrong adjustables of the 22 variety, but moved up to avoid damage by the springs and the greater axle movement now inbuilt by the other mods.

Ron Charlton's car had a TR4 petrol tank. He used Lotus Cortina 5½J wheels which were widened to 7″ at the front, and between 7½ to 8½ for the back. Ron used Goodyear Rallymaster Ultragrip for fast stage work, but preferred Dunlop Sp 44's on 4½ at the front and 5½ at the rear for sticky going. He used 13″ diameter wheels at all times. Although the discs at the front had competition pads installed, the GT rear brakes used standard linings to keep the handbrake efficient: Perdal also favour a servo with this set-up.

Mk. 1 Cortinas

There's no doubt that the King of Tweak must be Rod Cooper of Supersport Engines Limited, 64-66 Church Road, Acton, London, W3. Both he and his Team Supersport Cortinas won event after event a couple of seasons back—and what's more Rod seems to keep on winning on Escorts now. Although the Mk. 1 GT is different from the Mk. 1 Lotus in a number of respects apart from the obvious power unit differences and cost, Rod reckons on building up both types along the same lines, using the same know-how and most of the same bits. But first, along with most serious rally preparation outfits, Supersport take seriously minded customer's car completely to bits and start from scratch.

They strengthen and weld the body at the back where the shockers mount to the body. This needs double skinning really. They then, at the front, favour a bracing tube across from one turret to the other to stop the wings moving closer to each other on a really rough event. At the same time they weld cups into the shell for the struts to seat in, and double skin.

At the back, they use standard Mk. 1 Cortina GT springs with heavy-duty rubbers in the spring eyes. They then fit Armstrong Adjustaride 22's set at 15. If anyone has a very early Mk. 1 Lotus Cortina, Supersport do their rear-end leaf spring conversion for £46 18s. which is absolutely essential for rallying.

It pays off to fit an export cross-member which they can also supply. The anti-roll bar brackets ought to be double-skinned to prevent them bending back, and the thickest anti-roll bar is best. Supersport machine these bars to give the same castor angle as with a GT bar. Their suspension legs are vital too. These cost £11 per pair exchange, but for this you receive them wedged, uprated and long stroked. Heavy duty coil springs at £4 19s. 6d. should be fitted to any Mk. 1 too. Then you need special beefed up bump stops at 30s. a pair to fit on to the crossmember, but with exactly the right spacing to prevent the springs from becoming coil bound. It's the sort of attention on the suspension side of things that stop their shells from breaking up—even after several hard seasons' usage. A Lotus has far too low suspension legs at the front, so they too need these mods.

Rod doesn't personally like a servo, so he fits DS 11's at the front with the very important cooling slots in the pad surface that Ferodo Competitions do as part of their race/rally service for bona-fide entrants. At the rear, the almost standard wear on rally cars, VG 95's, are used. He uses the Goodyear Ultra-grip Rally Specials which are 175 type on 5½J Lotus steel wheels all round.

Mk. 2 GT and Lotus Cortinas

These can be treated along the same lines. The P16 calipers on both cars are all right as they are, obviously set up with DS 11 pads and VG 95s. The .7″ bore master cylinder combined with the .75″ rear wheel cylinders give the best braking performance for most events in this country.

As this is still the current model, there are many rallying tuning firms who are well qualified by personal experience with these popular weapons to set them up for you or supply the right bits for you to do the work yourself. Although rallying tuning firms make up quite a lot of their Cortina Mk. 2 tuning equipment, most items can be found in the Ford Performance Centre's lists. This equipment is definitely the genuine ex-works replica gear, so it can't be bad.

The ultimate in wheelery for the Mk. 2 is without doubt the Minilite in size 13 with 6″ rim width. These should be kitted out with Goodyear Ultragrips, or Goodyear G800s, according to the terrain—and even racing boots if it's that sort of event. For those who are a little pressed for the necessary, then it has to be steel. Go for the 5½J as on all Mk. 2 Lotus Cortinas, or rather Cortina Lotus.

34

If your Mk. 2 is going to be caned over roughery then you ought to achieve GT ride height. So this means uprated and wedged struts, plus a set of stiff springs up front. For the back, it's just a matter of changing over to comp. springs and Armstrong adjustable shockers. On fast and smooth thrashes, then go for a Lotus ride height with suitable springs—usually softer.

But don't take it out just like that yet. You do need a heavy-duty steering link. These are available through your Ford dealer from the Ford Performance Centre, and are now advisable as a result of somebody's painful experience in the past I wouldn't wonder! The HD steering link is really hard, having been specially heat-treated.

Still on the steering box end of things—why not fit a high ratio unit? This way, there will be no excuse for not being able to correct the unexpected deviation from the straight line round a stage, and apparently, with a high ratio box installed, driving glove life amazingly is increased. So this has to be a must.

If you can afford it, and you intend campaigning your Mk. 2 semi-seriously, you ought to strip the front suspension out of the shell and slot in a heavy-duty export type crossmember instead. With one of these vital components ensconced at the very heart of the shell, you'll find that there is no real need to alter the camber at all, as you'll have achieved 0 to 1 degree as an in-built feature. At the same time as this mammoth activity is going on, weld up around the strut housings and crossmember . . . that is if you want to avoid having to fork out for another one too soon.

Whilst on shell preparation for the Mk. 2, it is as well to ensure that,

even when the heavens open as they invariably do, you eliminate one of the most unpleasant rally happenings. This is when the water sprays and finally gushes, according to the depth of the no-goer, through the very thoughtfully positioned floor drain holes. These should be welded up as it's almost impossible to keep floor grommets in place for very long on a rally wagon, and in any case it's the only way to keep the inside of shells gunge-free.

As on all rally cars, try to put the pipery inside the shell. If you must keep it outside try to protect it with shields, or, on suspended runs, with rubber tubing. This can easily be split and taped over again when the vulnerable line or cable is safely inside the rubber sheathing. The Mk. 2 Cortinas that came out of Boreham all had wire springs round their brake hoses too.

Escorts

Escorts seem to be coming more and more numerous on every event these days. In 1300 GT form they are a very useful class potential, whilst the Twin Cam can win outright anywhere in the world. Alan Allard at the Allard Motor Company, Upper Richmond Road, Putney, uses an Escort himself, and therefore knows exactly how to set up any type of Escort.

The big pushrod-motor Escorts are only eligible for clubbies or Group 6 classes, but you can change over to Escort Twin Cam specification suspenders even on the 1300 GT as it's all homologated for Group 2. So whatever Escort is being used, change over to Escort Twin Cam brakes and the larger stub axles. The '68 model GT did not have roll bars fitted as standard, so you would need to have brackets bolted on to take a very necessary anti-roll bar. Different and stronger track control arms are really needed as well. Rally struts are almost standard equipment on rally Escorts—Allards do these at £18 10s. a pair. Turret conversions to stop things suddenly poking through the shell and the like are very wise. These sprout up into the boot and were homologated in the '69 Group 2—like most mods it would seem. These turrets permit vertical shockers and mean quite an expensive job involving fabrication of box sectioning as well as new parts. Allards do this work for around the £70 mark including all new bits. It's wise to include radius arms at the back to stop the back axle twisting and cut down the dreaded hop. Then there are rally springs, which increase ride height at the back by ¾" as well as making things suitably stiff. The necessary Armstrong adjustables are the same as on most modified Cortina GTs.

On the mini-Escort, the standard brakes at the back are quite good enough and only need VG 95s. At the front, whether you have TC bits or not, you should of course fit DS 11s. 12″ wheels ought to be altered to a set of 5½J 13s. For these, you'll have to flare the front wheelarches to give sufficient clearance, and also to cover the tread area at the side as the law demands —or something. Ford do an extension kit themselves to cover this plus-job, the bits cost £3 10s. for doing both sides. Again, the Goodyear Rally whatsits are O.K., and there's the almost universal Dunlop SP 44, which many Escort privateers like to use. It is possible to run on 5½J x 13 wheels with a maximum

tyre width of 165 mm without modifying front wheelarches—Allards know coz they've done it on Escort GTs.

Escort shells seem to weather all the punishment that Clerks of the Courses can organise, but they last that much longer if a certain amount of seam welding takes place first of all. Another plate should ideally be welded in place beneath the crossmember to ward off buckling over a hard season.

Getting the TC ready is about the same, except of course that the large brakes are standard. So you only need to change the struts over to rally ones, fit the track control arms and change to comp springs at £8 a pair exchange. No doubt the coil spring and re-located axle set up as introduced to us all on the '69 Clark Circuit car, used by Ove on the Welsh, will appear in kit form soon. Wheels are 5½J x 13 as standard, so problems in this department are over, unless one wants to go wider in the rim. But then the expensive body spot conversion would become necessary.

The Capri

This is very similar to Escort and Cortina, so before long, all the special bits that private owners might like to fit to their Capris should be available—if not through the Ford Performance Centre, then certainly through the mass of rallying Ford conversion concerns.

You can of course rally anything, and in that case if you don't like playing the part of Development Engineer of Motor Rallying—consult the Manufacturers, Concessionaires where applicable, or the Marque Specialists.

chapter 5

THE OFFICE

NOW let's take a look at an important interior aspect of the rally machine—the cockpit. Cockpit preparation is as vital as any other section of the rallying team, don't make it too much like the cab of a 707, or go the other way and make it all too simple. There is a great deal to be said for forgetting what the overall result of the cockpit looks like and go for functional efficiency.

Look at your dash as two sections. Firstly, the driver's side of things ought to have just the right instruments. He doesn't need a compass nor an altimeter; he doesn't need, nor should he have time to look at, too many temperature dials. A speedo is unimportant apart from legal necessity, but a rev counter, an oil pressure and a water temperature gauge are vital. These should be well illuminated and moved—within the regs that govern the category that you've entered your car in—so that they can be seen with the absolute minimum of taking one's eyes off the road. Some drivers like to have a rheostat fitted for dimming down the house lights in thick fog, or when driver fatigue is beginning to tell and a driver has to concentrate 100% on where he's going. But, even a luxury like this is something else to go wrong—so if you can do without such an extra, so much the better. There are also aircraft-type additional mini-lights on the market, which, being hooded for anti-glare, are very effective for efficiently high lighting vital instrument readings. They are fiddly to fit and wire neatly, but I have found them to be really useful on some works cars I have driven.

Switches

It helps to label switches clearly with "Dymotape". Most of the works teams do this, as any strange co-driver, who might have to move the car can find his way round the cockpit and comprehend the controls. It's also very useful, if you're absolutely knackered to be sure that you are in fact operating the right switch. But, it all boils down to keeping the layout and quantity of the switching down to an essential minimum.

The Navigator/Co-Driver side of the car ought to be kitted out with those services that he needs to be concerned with. He needs a Tripmaster from Halda, or one of the very excellent Gemini ones—and this ought to be illuminated separately, so that the Navigator can control whether he's a light on in this box or not. Here, it's as well to point out the obvious. He must be able to see the reading on the meter. So it must either be mounted as near to the navigator as is necessary or have a magnifier affixed to the unit's reading window. As on the driver's side, all the controls that concern the Navigator must be reachable— even they have to be moved with the belts on firmly. On some cars, once a change of front seats has been effected, the leg room at the front becomes converted from driving and passengering positions that are more suitable for legless dwarfs, to more like the fixed-type full harness stance that most Rallyists prefer. So, with belts done up, the basic controls are thus out of reach, or are at least very inconvenient to operate. Thus, it's a case of fitting bits of plastic tube, or switch extensions to the toggle switches, to bring them nearer to immediate hand. You can, in really bad cases, mount the switches out on raised up panels, or even move them into the centre on a console, or fit them into either side door pockets. The only snag with extending the loom out from the dash to such local switch sub-stations is that the wiring is more likely to become severed and the connections and switches with the doors opening and shutting are more likely to become shaken into open-circuiting. Then there's the problem, especially with door pocket switch layouts, of a clout against a bank causing a major firework party in that area. Floor mounted consoles often get in the way of sumpshield bolts and, if on a longer event the gearbox or the gearbox mountings need some attention, such a console and all the vital wiring could get in the way.

Mount everything as firmly as possible. Loose fitting self-tappers will only fall out on the rough, so go up a size of self-tapper to make sure a panel stays in place. On the other hand build your dash, so that at least it can be serviced easily. Just imagine what would happen if your dash panel was riveted in place and you just had to sit it out by the roadside till morning merely because a wire had slipped off your main lighting switch—maddening. Always prepare your cockpit so that it stays together—but can be worked on. Use the Lucas wiring master colour coding for your additional wiring, or evolve your own colour code, so that fault tracing on events can be easy. Naturally, solder all connections properly, using bullets and snaps. All wiring should be harnessed together in sub-runs for ease of car overhaul and inter-event servicing.

A fusebox for all the added auxiliaries should be included in your wiring, by merely running all switched feeds via the box before wiring out to the lamps or whatever. This fusebox ought to be labelled clearly too, and spare fuses taped into a ready position nearby.

Seeing the map

A navigator's flexible lamp is absolutely necessary. The Butlers' "Flexilight" is about the commonest in use. This swivels around to whatever position you want, being made of a spring like semi-rigid tubing. The chrome finish on these map lights can be very distracting, so matt black this out, as you should with all shiny chromey horrors, and this includes instrument bezels. On the subject of these lamps, two good tips to follow. Keep, or tape, a spare bulb for your lamp handy, so that in the very likely event of your light's bulb blowing just at the most crucial moment of an event—you are well prepared. The other point, that is well worth following, is to fit similar lights under the bonnet as well as in the boot, they're really useful when you're working in these darkest of dark areas. These lamps are available in 12″, 18″ and 30″ lengths—so all installations are well catered for. It's as well to fit in-line fuses in the runs to these service lights as we don't want any shorting near petrol.

Seats

The bucket seat on the driver's side should be very strong and fixed back type. It also ought to be fairly hard, so the driver can feel what's happening to his car through the seat of his pants. The navigator's seat really ought to recline, so, that on the longer events, one can kip. That's why you want a really uncomfortable driver's seat you see—to keep him awake! Both seats ought to be equipped with full harness safety belts. It's vital to ensure that these harnesses are correctly secured, so follow the instructions that are included with safety belts most carefully. They have been formulated through years of experience. The angle of the shoulder straps is usually the one that most people get wrong. But belts, seats, and whether headrests are fitted or not, are a purely personal affair. And the amazing variations in the top rally crews' seating/belt specifications speaks for itself as this aspect of car preparation is, perhaps more than any other, a purely personal interpretation.

Steering wheels are all a matter of personal choice, too. Standard ones are fine with gloves. Woodrim are not such a good idea in a shunt, and the best are padded leather rimmed ones. They usually buckle well in a shunt, and you don't get skewered with a busted rim or detached spokes.

The screenwasher ought to be electric, if it isn't already. The reservoir ought to be a reasonable size and moved into the cockpit if the regs allow it. Tudor do some very good washer kits for the do-it-yourself rallyist. It helps if this washer can be actuated by driver or navigator, so two switches, or at least a central one, are a good idea.

A grab handle for the navigator to steady himself with is a good plan—he'll appreciate it anyway.

Safety

Fire extinguishers for both sides of the cockpit are vital, not only to finish rallies, but also to save the car—and all the work too—from going up in smoke. There is undeniably a certain fire risk in rallying, so be prepared.

You don't want all your hours of midnight oil burning—not that this is quite the right word—going up in smoke. Invariably fire damage to an interior or underbonnet area spells write-off—just as much as a really good old bender into a tree does.

No doubt, before very long, most rally cars will have aircraft-type fire extinguisher systems as are fitted to most racing cars nowadays. These are either temperature excess actuated or can be banged on by the crew, if fire breaks out in the engine compartment. But then, after all, if all pipes and wires are really secure, a fire shouldn't break out in the first place.

On the safety side of cockpit preparation too, a roll cage, really well braced and padded, is a must. Not only will a bar inside protect the crew members in an inversion, but it will also help to save the basic shape of any shell, which can amazingly mean that panel beating is all that is required after a shunt instead of a new bodyshell. All very gloomy—but rally accidents do happen. That is if you try!

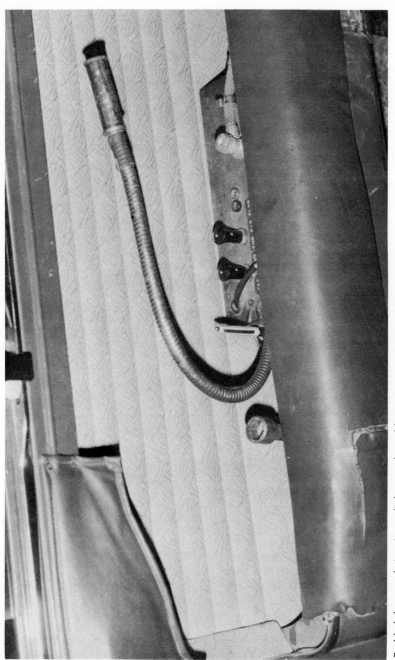

Padded door pocket, extra switch console and boom type navigation light complete the co-driver's side of the office. This car is an ex-works Mini Cooper 'S'.

If you have to take a whole lot of gear along, then batten everything down. Here's a Coburn Viva boot all set for an upside down stage.

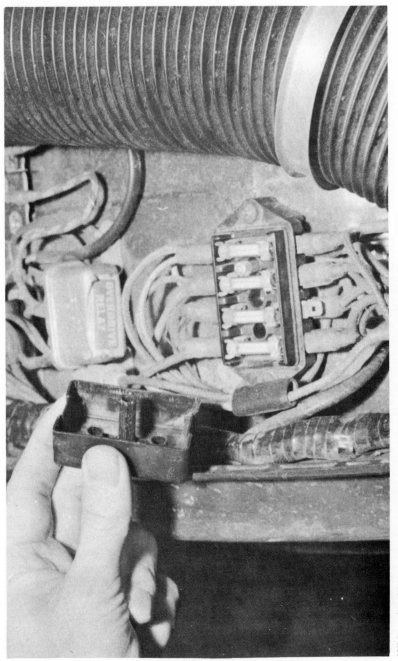

Wiring should be as neat as this beautiful loom. All circuits are fused separately, relays protect all switched circuits, and all wires are colour coded.

Simple and uncluttered, with everything labelled and to hand, this is Colin's '68 Championship winning Imp's fascia.

chapter 6

LIGHTING THE WAY

CERTAIN annual talking points at any Motor Club are the many theories on how to improve one's standard lighting lot. Naturally as most rallying takes place in the dark.

The MOT, needless to say, has been active of late over revising the lighting regs. The very imposing "Road Vehicles (Headlamps) Regulations of 1968" require that from Jan. 1st, headlamps as well as side lights must be used on most vehicles moving at night on all slots outside lit areas. They do concede that, when it's foggy, fogs can be used instead of heads. Thankfully this should make the phantom practice of the candlelit gnome, progressing in anonymous folly, disguised as a pair of semi-defective sidelights or a motorbike wrapped in a patch of fog, illegal. The MOT wise ones have not decreed when either mainbeam or heads should be used, for as we all know full well this varies with circumstances. Ministers Marsh and Mulley who at least hold driving licences, saith that in fog two fog lamps, or a fog and a spot lamp, mounted symmetrically, and within a distance of 16″ of the outer edges

of the vehicle, are necessary if they are to be used instead of headlamps. So it was made to come to pass, that until 31st of December '69 you were allowed to use one fog instead of headlamps. Another factor for the motor manufacturers to consider is that all cars registered for the first time on or after the 1st of January '71 will have to comply as follows: fogs, if used instead of heads, will have to be symmetrically positioned within 16″ of the outer edges of the coachwork.

It's meant that officially an awful lot of rallyists' lamps have had to be repositioned so that they are now within these rules, and, what's more, pairs have had to be made up too.

One brand that seems to be very regularly in evidence, certainly amongst the Rallying fraternity anyway, is Cibié. The backbone of the range, and well know to all enthusiasts, is the Oscar. This can be obtained for £7 15s., in either fog, long range or driving form. The ordinary Oscar is 162 mm, whilst Cibié also supply Fords with the scorching Oscar BB, which is 200 mm in lens diameter, though Ford owners have to order this from the Ford Performance Centre, Boreham. Then there's the slim Cibié, type 45, for those who have insufficient depth to fit the Oscar. Like the Oscar, the 45 is fitted with 55w H1 quartz-iodine bulb. The 45 is stainless steel, very slim and comes with a plastic stone and shunt shield, for £7 15s. For the rectangular market, there's the new ultra compact type 35, in fog or long range. It has the H2 bulb, still 55w though, with a smaller cap, which has become necessary with a lamp as shallow, yet with increased reflective area. The sack on the Philips H2 is the same, it's the bayonet fixing that's so minute. The 35 can be mounted either way up—and comes with a lens shield for £6 14s. 6d.

Conversions

As with most lamp makers these days, Cibié cater for those rallyists who want to transform their standard headlight units instead of (or in addition to) fitting extra fog/drive/spot lamps. Their type 22, which can be dip right or left merely by sliding a lever on the back of the unit, is supplied complete with bulbs, connectors and instructions for a DIY installation for £6 12s. 6d. As there are very few standard headlamps that are truly proficient for instant rallying, conversion by a change of light unit is a priority in lighting preparation. However, star of the range is the Biode. This is in direct competition with Marchal's units that have been out on the market for some time, though the dipped and main beam bulbs on the Cibie are happily interchangeable. The bulbs are H1s, the price £17 complete, although you are advised to spend a further £1 11s. on a relay. Biode—French for two iodines—has two

reflectors in one light unit, each reflector and bulb perfect for its job of dip or main beam. If you want to be really demon with the lights, they can be wired so both dip and main happen at the same time when mainbeam is selected. Very shortly, Biodes will be available as for Peugeot's 204 size of rectangular lamp with one of the sides extended by a circular segment. These units you may have spotted on some of the works Escorts lurking behind perspex shields in their prototype form. Soon Viva, Escort and Hunter owners will be able to go over to Biode when a further pure rectangular offering arrives.

There is no point in spending hard earned bread on a lovely set of lamps if you go and feed them via a Heath Robinson wire up. One works prepared car had bits of house wiring for its auxiliary loom, whilst another had all its accessories fed off the instrument panel lights !

Dipping QI's

Mazda have made a worthy contribution to the lighting world of late with their dipping quartz halogen bulb, which has 55w main beam and 43w dip. It's claimed to give off a beam intensity twice as powerful as a conventional bulb. The filaments are coiled tungsten. The evaporated tungsten from the hot filament reacts with the halogen that's sealed in the bulb's envelope. The result is halide. The high temperature of the filament breaks up the halide, redepositing the tungsten onto the filament, and, at the same time, releasing the halogen to repeat the cycle. The bulb is fully interchangeable with bulbs in BPF standard light units. At least in many cases you can still use your existing light units and there's also no

A neat lamp arrangement. This one is Simo Lampinen and John Davenport's SAAB V4 on the 1968 Rally. If they mean the Oscar's to be on – they have forgotten to uncover them!

problem with having to rig up extra and/or separate sidelights (as on the special twin Ql bulbed light units where they are not incorporated). Even sealed beams can be changed for the traditional standard metal/glass light units and adaptors for the sealed beam "prong" plugs. The dipping bulbs are 42s. 6d., with 7s. 5d. on top for another evil PT contribution.

One firm which specialises in lighting conversions is Epic Accessories. They offer a dipping tungsten halogen bulbed conversion with 7″ diameter light units for £7 a pair, and £7 10s. a pair with sidelight facility. They then do upped output sealed beams; 60/45s. for Mk. 2 Mins with sidelight for £2 15s. a pair, 60/45s. for £2 15s. a pair, and 75/50s. for £3 a pair. Their conversion for the VW prior to the later upright headlamped model is £12 10s. For this, you get better light units' wiring and all the connections. Epic do kits for 12 or 6v with 45/40w. The prices quoted are inclusive of carriage. Latest addition to their range is their 12v 75/60w or 6v 60/45w bulb for 25s. It simply replaces the bulbs used in most Continental cars and the GB rectangular light units.

Lucas have gone into modifying headlamps too. They can convert a four headlamp set-up with two separate sets of 5¾″ lamps, at £7 10s. a pair. Each set comprises of an appropriately lensed pair of light units with 55w QH bulbs. This set is in fact already an optional extra for the Aston DBS but is now on general release. Their new 7″ light unit kit costs £11 a pair, again the 60/55w QH being used from Philips, known in the trade as the duplo PH 4. The Lucas range has something for everyone—and spares are available everywhere.

Sound connections

Whatever lamps you fit, here are a few basic points to ensure that you follow. Don't skimp on the wiring or the connection. Use good quality bullets and insulated connectors—especially if the lamps might have to come off periodically to get at some mechanical component for servicing. Use good wire. Use grommets on all the holes. Tape the wire sensibly to relatively stationary items to stop it flapping about. Use an auxiliary fuse board or box if you're fitting extra lights up—at very least, use in-line fuse capsules. Try to make extra lights as thief proof as possible. Use lock nuts on lamp spigots—and why not a burglar alarm to protect your valuable goodies? Have all lights set up on a beam setter, the garage door or wall aiming went out with the ark. Replacement lenses are mighty expensive, so fit covers or guards in the day to ward off stones. A sturdy detachable lamp bracket, hinged where engine or front end maintenance accessibility is vital, is a good plan.

Relays

Finally, never fight shy of relays. They safeguard switch life and are a must to ease the burden of micro-contact switches that have been overloaded with extra lights. Column switches should always be protected by the insertion of relays in the wiring if a more powerful headlamp conversion is being fitted and the switching from dip to mainbeam is likely to increase the sparking at the contacts. If you can put up with more involved wiring, relays on all light switches will increase the reliability factor.

chapter 7

WHAT TO TAKE

THERE are two very contrasting mistakes that beginners to rallying always stand a pretty good chance of making. Either they clutter their machine up with everything but the kitchen sink, or they come unstuck because they run out of water. What to take along on an event, and what to leave behind in the garage? One of the most difficult aspects of preparation on which to generalise or on which to make any hard and fast rules. If I tell you that experience is the only real criteria, then I'm not really making a complete guide to rallying. But it's only by making your own mistakes in taking along too much or too little, that you'll ever finally arrive at the ideal amount of gear to get you to the end of an event.

If you want to win a sprint event, where the margin between the first few cars is likely to be very very slim, then you naturally ought to be weight conscious to the extreme. After all, you'll probably not even be able to afford the time to clean your screen—that is if you want to win. The only real reason on a tight night rally to take along any bits at all is to

make the job of being able to patch the car up to get it home easier. Spares, although taking up room and adding weight, might, in such a case, prove to be a great saver of time and expense, in that a tow car need not have to be called to the scene of retirement from the other end of the country to get you mobile.

Weight and Space

But, convenience of recovery apart, the two factors to consider are weight and space. Both these factors have to be looked at, according to what sort of banger you're using. Having decided on what you're taking along, you then have to spend a great deal of time scientifically determining where you are going to put this and that. Packing a rally car up is quite time consuming. There's no use putting something you're going to use quite frequently at the bottom of a whole pile of gear that is likely to be very rarely called for, and then having to waste valuable competing time burrowing through a mound of unimportant spares to get at what you're after. Again you want everything in its place, according to the sort of priority of call you're likely to encounter. And a place for everything. Both crew members, and indeed all helpers on the event, ought to know where everything is stowed. If you're using new support crew members, or a new navigator, then they ought to have been given a conducted tour before the event. Time is what rallying is all about, so you don't want to just give it away to the other competitors. For preparation of what you take along as spares of one kind or another is every bit as important as preparation of the car itself. The stowage places ought to be chosen so that each item can be extracted with the minimum of effort, yet that item ought to be really securely fastened down. Either oddment compartment can be constructed, of a permanent nature if you're dedicated enough, with securable flap lids to contain items within their confines, or custom-made clips can be fitted for each part. Those elasticated luggage to luggage rack thongs, with a hook at either end, are very useful for stringing about the car to secure awkward items, and stop helmets rolling about. One of those octopus straps can be a boon as a web inside a boot. You don't want all your bits and pieces cascading around the inside of anywhere. For a start, you'll damage them or the rest of the car and secondly you'll not be able to find anything when you want it in a hurry. It's as well also to stow everything with the safety of the crew in mind, too. A trolley jack wanging into the backs of your heads on a violent yump is not the best way to avoid a rally headache. Place the essential bits in the car so that if the car rolled, all doesn't get lost. Not that one plans definitely

to roll, but one never knows, and preparation for the shunt is one of the finer points of packing bits and bobs in place.

Different vehicles are known to consume different sorts of parts, so known dodgy bits should be carried, if the event's distance is going to chance the particular part's luck. On Marathon events, the carrying of most of the potentially required spares is important. Servicing will, by nature of the geographical spread of such routes, be few and far between, so the crew will have to provide most of the spares from their boot. They'll also have to be carrying the right tools for the job. Where service is likely to be at the end of every stage, there's little point in emulating the Parts Stores of your local Main Dealer. Again, specific events will demand specific equipment. So, for a snow-covered Monte, you'd need to carry a de-drifting shovel and some serated boards to extricate the car from a position of zero traction. If you had to traverse a flooded swamp region, you'd obviously carry a winching device to get the car through. But, it would be foolish to clutter your efforts up with such specialised aids on a mid-summer half-nighter in Buckinghamshire.

Experience, the individual event, the intentions of the crew to get through or to win, or both ; all factors in the decision-making necessary to finalise what ought to fill the door pockets and boot. But do secure everything really well, and be sure to consider that it's all weight, which will in turn affect the performance of the vehicle, as well as increasing the work and possibly reducing the reliability of the suspension. Having decided what you're going to pack into the car, make a check list, so that, prior to the type of event, you can be sure that nothing is forgotten. This checking off can be combined with cleaning and servicing the parts and tools to be carried, for they have just as tough a time as many of the parts on the rally car itself.

The need for spare oil, brake fluid and water is fairly obvious. But one tip I have found useful is to carry only those spanners which fit items on the car which you know you may have to work on. Tools weigh plenty, and there is no point in taking along ones that you're not likely to use. One often sees competitors rummaging through a great tin chest full of what should be clipped neatly to their workshop tool racks in search for the right spanners to effectively tighten a fanbelt. De-icer and ignition water repellent are vital door pocket potions, as is some radiator sealing goo—so often forgotten. But don't overdo it, or else the pocket or glove box will look too much like a shop shelf.

On a forestry rally, where punctures are going to become more likely, two spare wheels should be carried. But even here, if there's going to be a service car at the end of every stage there's little point in taking two. For if you do get a puncture on a stage, two things will invariably have happened, you'll have ruined the tyre anyway before (and if!) you've stopped to change the wheel. And if you have done even a snappy wheel change on the stage, you'll have done such a lousy time that you'll not be too worried about that particular bit of the rally any more. For the very private owners, having two spare wheels and tyres is certainly conducive to a happier state of mind for the driver. So, here again the final choice is a personal one. And the only ruling I can make is to say how important it is to ensure that the wheels stay battened down and don't break adrift. For a loose studded tyre can do an awful lot of damage to petrol tanks, piping and pumps—not to mention wear and tear, on the wiring.

Servicing

Coupled with what you take with you in the car goes servicing. Servicing is a fine way of getting to know a great deal about rallying. Fast and safe road driving of the service car, accurate navigation, the art of bodging up a car so that it can be made mobile as soon as possible, preventative maintenance and knowing as much about every nut and bolt of the rally car being serviced as the car's crew itself—is the name of the game.

The service car has to be chosen carefully. It has to be prepared and packed as proficiently as the rally car. It has to be reliable, and it has to take one helluva hammering. Most of the leading private owners have their own regular crews who could give most of the middle field competitors a run for their money, fully laden with welding bottles and the like too. In a service car you need, as well as rally experienced personnel, one or more top class mechanics. And so, outside the ranks of those actually competing, you've got quite a job to find sufficiently experienced enthusiasts. If you do have a service car, then it's fairly obvious that it should take most of the weight. And if most of the major parts and tools are in the service car, then it's equally vital that the rally car driver knows exactly where he's likely to expect to rendezvous with his service crew.

The itinerary of the service crew must be realistic, but yet with the maximum possible frequency. This is one of the many jobs of the navigator/co-driver.

The raw novice may be a little worried as to how he will ever be able to afford to gather together whole lumps of suspension and spare this and that, that is when he sees the sort of sophisticated gear some of the top competitors' service crews carry about with them. Well, the more rallying you do, the more part-worn spares you'll find you'll accumulate. For it's obvious that it's so much better to change worn parts on a rally motor before they break, and before long you'll find you'll be blessed with whole sections of your motor car in duplicate. These parts are quite good enough to carry as spares. Then there's also sale or return on parts from your local and, if you pay your bill, friendly garage. Perhaps if you get to know them really well, welding tackle, ramps and a trolley jack could be persuaded to wander away from the garage— just for the rally. And who knows, you may even land up with a sponsor this way.

chapter 8

MARSHALS - THE UNSUNG HEROES

THE drivers and navigators usually star in rallies, as of course do the cars. Very little is ever said about the marshals. In all weathers, the marshal is the essential accessory for any rally organisers.

For anyone who fancies the idea of ever having a go at rallying, marshalling is an ideal first introductory step. You'll see plenty of mistakes as a marshal, and above all you can see whether you're going to really like rallying. It's not all beer and skittles. It's mighty expensive, and can be frightfully disappointing at times. As a marshal for a while, you'll be able to sample rallying without being irretrievably financially involved. If you like what you see, you can then have a go.

Marshalling involves every basic skill of any rallyist : be they navigator or driver. So often the marshal has to compete in his own private rally to make his control points on time. If he's going to be any good at marshalling, or let's say make a professional job out of it, he'll no doubt conscientiously prepare himself and equipment for his Saturday night's work. Marshalling involves preparation of equipment, mastering paperwork, driving fast and safely, map reading, and organisation. He also has to be very resilient to the ravings of the Prima Donna type of navigator, who will argue vehemently if the right time just happens to be the wrong time for his purposes. But you've just got to be 100% enthusiastic to put up with, and master, the range of problems that a marshal can encounter over a season's rallying. Another point to remember is that regrettably it's going to cost you. You may get your breakfast—often two tickets—at the finish Hotel, but that's about the extent of it. So it goes without saying that a night's motoring in Wales, especially travelling to and from your home to Wales, isn't cheap.

There's no better way to get the bug than to be waiting at your control point halfway up a mountain in the middle of the night, listening to, and watching the approach of a string of rally cars hammering up a valley towards your point. Their lights flashing in the sky, and occasionally illuminating the hillside all round, their exhausts screaming up and down the scale with gear-change after gearchange crunching home, their tyres screeching and wailing in protest, their brake lights banging on and off like fairy lights, and their sumpshields graunching the tarmac after the humps—it's got to be exciting. Then in they come, spread out, or in groups, all dicing like merry hell. After you, they then thrash on into the night with boot-fuls of oil haze, exhaust smoke and torn rubber dust—on to their next point. So you're already hooked?

You may think that marshalling is child's play. It might seem like merely writing down times on bits of paper. Sutton and Cheam Motor Club member, David Jones, who's graduated from being marshal into actually having a go at navigating in Tony Fowkes' Lotus Cortina, thought just this. He was wrong.

David applied to a local Motor Club, which was putting on a Restricted event, to marshal a time control, saying that he'd had pre-vious experience of manning a time control. He had caught the bug before this by going to help a group of pals marshal a control on another event, but had spent most of that time watching all the motoring rather than mastering the system. He was promptly given rather an important control on a long loop, which was very tight, accuracy being naturally very important for the organisers. David received the exact location and time from the Club during the week leading up to the event. He arrived at the point with a car load of friends, and settled down to await the arrival of the sector opening marshal with his points clock, boards, flag, and bundle of cards. After the board was erected about fifteen feet from the car, and the flag a further fifty feet

beyond, the Jones party settled down to await the first visiting car. The first car screamed up with the second and third cars right on its heels. What a mess. They hadn't put down their control's number on their cards, or indeed signed them even. By the time they emerged sleepily from the warmth of their car to deal with this first batch of competitors, the competitors were naturally be-coming rather irate. They continued to fiddle about, getting more and more in a state as the field went by. They had made mistakes too, easily done, but mistakes. They had read out times from the clock, written down the times that the competitors had been shouting at them, and then luckily put the correct time of arrival/ departure down on their master check sheet. Luckily for David, someone had been diligently keep-ing an accurate master check sheet in the car, so the organisers were able to be furnished with the real timings of their control point, and not some of the times that had appeared on the cards that the competitors had been given and which they in had turn handed to the organisers at the finish of the rally. Lesson number two—don't take any notice of the time a navigator may shout up. The better the navigator, the more con-vincing will be his performance.

You'll have to join a motor club that either runs rallies itself or at least gets plenty of invitations to compete in other clubs' events. Then/or you write to the Secretary of each rally asking him to send you a set of regulations for that event. In the regs will be a form for those who wish to marshal to fill in. In-variably, you'll then have to send this form back to the Chief Marshal. If you've not had any previous ex-perience, then you'll most probably be given a passage check to man as opposed to a time control. At a passage check, all you'll have to do is either sign all visiting competitors' road books or merely give them one of your passage check's cards to prove that they've visited you. They then hand in all their cards at the end of the rally and so the results are worked out.

Choose the better events, and go for the ones that offer free breakfast. You'll find that there's so much to learn at a rally breakfast anyway. For the first time, tag onto the back of regular marshals and learn the ropes. Then have a go at a passage check on your own. A passage check can be mighty hairy at times, with cars screaming upon you in batches. Keep your head, don't panic, and don't be bullied by the competitors.

No birds

David Jones is adamant about the equipment that you need to take with you when you're marshalling. You need an alarm clock for one— yes I expect you thought you'd never need that on any rally. An alarm clock is very useful to wake you up well before the first car is due, so that you're really wide awake for the wiles of those navigators. Then strong, reliable, and duplicated lighting gear is needed, such as a Hurricane or Tilly lamp, as well as a good torch—with plenty of spare batteries, coz the shops are closed you see. Warm and waterproof clothing is essential, even though it's not all that chilly out back in the smoke, when you take Fido for a walk. But meanwhile, a hundred miles or more away on top of a Welsh mountain, it can be a very different meteorological situation— like would you believe blowing half a gale at just about freezing! Don't

take your Bird because relations will only become strained, being kept up all night, getting plastered with mud every time a car rushes off up the track, freezing cold, and not really being able to compete with the rally cars as far as gaining a fella's full attention. David suggests that four people are best, with duties as follows. One will have to keep a check list. This lucky orderly soul ought to be ensconced in the warmth of the car so that at least his office is one sheltered place on the mountain where things are likely to stay dry and not get blown away. Then, when the cars start to be due to appear, the other three should stand about ten feet apart, in order to stuff cards through the rally cars' windows. They should be spread out each with a biro and torch, so that wherever a car stops in the queue, that car at least gets a passage card or a signature immediately. It then means that a convoy will at least still be on equal terms when they leave the control. Then the next thing to do clearly, and very loudly if it's a rough rally and the odd silencer box is getting a little woofly, is to call out the number of the car that is being done, as the check card is handed over. Naturally, it'll be very difficult on occasions to see what the number is at all, because of all the mud that seems to cling to all numbers, including—some say happily—the number plate. So as soon as the car comes to a stop at the control scream out—"Number please?" Do this before the navigator starts trying to get things done his way.

Control

The next step—if you're still interested—is to have a go at a time control. Start off with a smaller event, as it's not really fair to be a newcomer to marshalling on a top class event like one of the events that count towards the M.N. Championship. Again, four people are needed really. One can then read the watch, one can write the check sheet, though this time times will have to go down as well by each competitor. The others can hand out the time cards and write the number and time on each one, as they hand one to each car.

David tells me that accuracy is the most important thing. With time controls, be sure to read the watch particularly carefully. One minute either way—and the whole result of a rally may be affected, indeed a Championship might change dramatically as a result of what one marshal does. So each marshal is a very important cog in the rallybox. Always be prepared to show the competitor the time clock if he wants to see it—a lot will do.

Obviously be firm with the right time and resist putting down the time that is called up by the navigator. Again, if the time required is later than the time shown on the clock, then the car must be held until the minute comes up on the clock. At both time and passage controls, a direction of approach will be specified. Should a car approach from a wrong direction, give him a time but be sure to mark WD (wrong direction) in large letters next to the time on the time card, or on his Road Book, if it's one of those rallies. Then also mark WD on your master sheet, so the organisers have a double chance of penalising the competitor.

Gate Marshal

You may find yourself as a gate marshal. This may sound a frightfully humble task—but it's just as important. A gate marshal keeps the local farmer happy, and the local farmer needs to be happy if his lovely muddy pot-holed farm tracks are going to be able to be used on future rallies. Often livestock has to be prevented from wandering from one part of a farm to another. One stray cow can cost a great deal of club revenue to replace and it's always the best cow in the herd that wanders off on rally night. In any case, a stray animal on the road could wreck a rally car, as well as a crew too. When the time allowance is up for the last car, close the gate firmly, replacing chains, etc.

Closing up

When it's time to close the control and go home or to breakfast, after the course closing marshal has been through and collected your check sheet, don't leave any litter about. Remember that there's always another rally likely to be using the same piece of road in the future, so it helps to have left everything clean and tidy, so the farmer can have no objection to another rally passing. Marshals are very much in the local public's eye. So a good efficient show is a must. It's likely to aggravate the natives a great deal, if a marshal's post turns into a barbecue or an open air booze-up.

Quiet zone marshals have the future of rallying, as we know it today in this country, in their hands. If you're given a quiet zone to administer, then park your car outside the zone for a start, and you'll most probably be told to park out of sight of the competitors too. Competing cars are usually told to traverse these zones in a high gear, with dipped lights. Don't hold the poor old competitor to the letter of the rule here, but use your discretion.

A quiet zone has been made a quiet zone for a very good reason. The organisers on their pre-rally visits to all householders, on or near to the route, have most probably found an anti-rally Gnomelet. You must take the offending car's number, registration number if you can read it, make, model, and colour, if possible. An offender will always deny that it was he, who did a wheelie in Llanbogwiggy and let fly with his quadruple air horns at the vicar's cat, before hand-braking round on a JP's herbaceous thingy-meslips. Should you be confronted by an irate local, be as polite as possible despite the odd lunge you may have to parry off from a walking stick or club. Try to explain what's going on, and that it's all been authorised by the Police. If you still cannot seduce peasants with your charm—then give them the name and address of the secretary of the rally, as well as that of the clerk of the course, prior to retreating quietly.

Special stages

Then there are special stages and selectives. These have to be timed by marshals to the second, and so need even more special watches than the road section. These can also be read a minute out. On well organised events, marshals will have to control the public, as well as being dotted about along the stage-side to marshal arrowed junctions and really dangerous hazards, the speeds are very high, and things can break on the cars. Keep the public away from the outside of the corners. Make sure that they don't stand on the apex on the inside of a corner— as some drivers love to take short cuts. Try to educate the public in as friendly a fashion as possible. Many

of them may not have seen a rally before, and they won't therefore appreciate things in quite the same way as the hard core would do. Keep them from walking across the track with their backs towards the oncoming rally cars.

Standard procedures

If any organisers are with us at this point, it might not be out of place to make a plea here to standardise marshalling procedures. David Jones put forward a very sound plan. Each marshal's crew must be given very explicit instructions, bearing in mind that many crews will not be able to attend any briefings. On the instructions should be a complete list of black spots— areas where rallying is banned by the RAC as a result of past complaints—out-of-bounds areas applicable to the specific event, plus quiet areas, so that the marshals don't go belting through dodgy villages. In addition, the telephone numbers of the start, halts, and finish, which should be manned at all times. Then the exact map reference should be given of the point or points for the experienced adventurers, with a small diagram of the control's location, to avoid the marshals setting up shop off-plot slightly. Each control should have enough room for the marshal's car, at least one competitor who is being dealt with—as well as any other competitor who's likely to approach horribly out of control all crossed up under braking. If possible, an organiser ought to reward marshals with a pair of breakfast tickets, and, if the event is blessed with a very generous sponsor, then something towards petrol might not be a bad idea either. Marshals should all gather at a central meeting point before the event, close to the start, so that they can at least get a look at the competing cars at close quarters and talk to some of the crews.

Collecting the gear

Each marshal's crew should collect at this meeting his boards, flags, cards and check sheets, for every control they are going to man. The sector marshal should be responsible for all hazard and OK boards to be in position, and to see that all controls are manned. If they're not, he can then detail one of the spare marshal crews that he should have organised to follow him, to drop off and take over the unmanned point.

It can now be seen that a marshal should also have a well-prepared car too, which is reliable, suitably equipped with lights and the right tyres to travel to and return from the appointed point. Being a Sector marshal is as near as dammit like being on a rally.

chapter 9
DRIVING

IN so many cases there is far too much emphasis on making the car go like the clappers and not nearly enough thought on whether the disappointing rate of progress along the lanes is due to the driver's lack of self-analysis and rectification of his bad habits. Have a good think at what you are actually doing whenever you think you are really motoring down the whites. Are you in too low a gear? Are you looking far enough ahead? Are you braking for no reason? Are you using all the road that you can find?

The vast majority of Clubmen scream along in second cog, jerking their way round imaginary corners in between great bootfuls of brake pedal. So think about what you are doing, correct your technique, and then work on making what you do entirely natural. Only when you start pulling max revs in top down every straight bit is it time to wonder about the car's gearing or indeed making the motor make a few more revs even. It also goes without saying that a great deal of practice is necessary—and you're never ever perfect! You must always be pre-

pared to learn some more as the art of rally motoring is so much more difficult than all the racing types say it is.

There are really four distinct types of motoring that a driver has to deal with in the course of a series of rallies. First of all there is the liaison motoring on public roads between Special Stages, when the timing is very generous. Don't dawdle. Don't exceed the average speed blanketed on the road section by the organisers. Preserve the car—but above all stay out of trouble from the Police as well as other road users. Try not to draw attention to your passage. After all, the less people that are aware of the passage of a rally the better, until the results are splashed about the papers. And the better it is for the preservation of the sport. The more gnomes that try to buzz the competitors, the more locals that get buzzed by the competitors as well as by the rally followers—the worse becomes the image of rallying.

Don't draw attention to yourself, you are after all competing against the organisers and the other competitors—and not the general public or the local constabulary. On the bit about hanging about, remember that every minute you can save on the road means that you can spend this time servicing the needs of the motor car as well as those that nature demands from the crew! So the whole skill is to waste no time—but spare that car. Quick times on a gentle road section don't mean anything at all in the final analysis, especially as you only have the bar dwellers to impress in the nearest local to where you broke down!

Secondly, there are those occasions, usually after the midnight hour, when it's time to go like the clappers on a road section of a typical Club rally route. Every second is precious, although timing is to the whole minute. The average is supposed to be 30 m.p.h. and to sort the entry out there will be no time for anyone to relax. Now naturally if the whole rally just consists of a road section to sort the entry out, then maximum effort will be needed with the pressure well and truly on all the time. However, don't overdo the effort bit or you'll find that all you'll want to do after an hour or so is to have a long kip. It's so easy for a racing or sprint type approach to be applied to the night rally. You've got to pace yourself so that you last the exact distance of the event. There's no earthly use at all in arriving at breakfast in such a healthy and lively state that you have a surplus of energy to demolish a dozen breakfasts as well as having more strength in hand after lugging all the inevitable trophies back to your lair. The idea must be to spend yourself in the same way as a long distance runner does, so that you arrive at the finish and collapse into a deep sleep without your actual driving performance being affected

at all. Naturally where there are Stages or Sections timed to the second—or at a higher average speed—then you have to adjust your pace accordingly. But in any case try to achieve this perfect state of driver performance. It is just as important as preparing the car right.

As rallying is moving more and more towards the specially timed section on private property, then more and more attention should be given to driving where it really matters. Sections specially timed were thrown into a rally cocktail in the old days, for fun, for spectators, or to decide ties—so if anything the specialised techniques used in the bad old days were really in the main Driving Test ones, or rather Autotest manoeuvres.

Special stages

Eventually, road sections of the good old Welsh thrash may regrettably become a great rarity, most probably through public opinion and ultimate legislation, if nothing else. So the art of special stage driving has become an essential ingredient to success.

Where there is no local knowledge and where there are no notes being fed to you by your co-pilot it's all up to your ability to cope with whatever hazard lies over the next brow. Natural ability, speedy corrective reactions and looking way ahead are all very helpful. But the most important thing is to learn how to master the loose surface vices of your motorcar—and use those vices and shortcomings to the only advantage that really matters, and that is to get to the end of every stage in a rally in the shortest possible time.

The last type of hairy motoring that will come· the way of every rallyman is the continental section or selective, as it's labelled in most GB road books. Here, if it's public road, it's likely to be very hairy indeed, timed to the nearest second, and over the most testing and remote roads that the organisers can find. It could be loose surface—or broken surface—but is in most cases likely to be tarmac mountain thrash with a corner for every blink and a hairpin over every brow. Here "get-out-and-get-in-trouble-fast" techniques will be very important, but you'll have to adopt some race track style—certainly the racing line where it's wide enough. Care should be taken not to scrub off too much speed with too much excessive throwing it sideways at the hint of a bend. Lock should be scientifically applied, and, where possible, the car should be set up in a drift before the next corner. Unlike loose surface going, setting up the car before an unseen bit of road should be avoided. For there's no earthly use having your motor all tweaked up for a left-hander, when the rise in the road turns the other way and shoots into a right-hander, which was flat anyway.

The Swedish style of setting a car up the other way for corners which can be judged accurately in advance, and indeed using the sliding ability of the car to cope with whatever happens to the road next—because you couldn't possibly slow down with the brakes in the racing and conventional manner in time—shouldn't be exploited on a tarmac surface that is dry and free from ice or mud. You'll only scrub off an awful lot of your hard-won speed, wear the tyres out at a colossal rate and reduce your poor navigator to all sorts of bad passenger habits. The peace in your car can be shattered as a result—and serves you

right too, if you cannot open the window to allow the natural escape of his last meal! Mind you, hurling the car around on the throttle is all fun with a whole lot of power—but quite frankly it only impresses any action-hungry natives who might be squatting on the hillside bordering a section.

There is one other sort of driving that you may have to get up to during a rally and that is a section round a racing circuit. I feel that it's as well at this point to discuss certain aspects of race driving that will be of use to any rallyman in getting round any bit of tarmac road a little faster. The tips here though are only really of prime use if you know what comes next.

The main thing to master on the second lap is which gear to select for each corner. You will I hope know full well where the power comes in on your particular power pack. If you have found on your exploratory "driving unseen" first lap that you are suddenly being sapped to the bottom of your power band in the gear that you would have thought was ideal for a particular bend or series of bends, then down shift. In practice, quite honestly, forget all the theoretical guff about not changing down in the middle of corners or indeed not braking in the middle of turns. Concentrate on keeping all systems go within the limits of the indicated figures on your instruments, and keep the m.p.h. up to the absolute max. There's no use in getting the line right, being in the right gear, if it's all happening too slowly. Never be caught waiting for revs to build up until you are well and truly on the cam again. Also the higher the gear when the cam isn't near the peak—or rather the further off peak power you are—then the less the pull is likely to be and the less safe your progress through a bend as a result.

While you can, remember any key landmarks around a circuit. Go for something that you can readily pick out. Marks on the road are quite good sometimes when you are going too fast to be able to pick out a flag pole from one helluva lot of blurred scenery each lap. Changes in road surface or joins in the tarmac are of use too. Build up to your ultimate braking point as quickly as possible, but don't overstep this as we don't want to hold everyone else up on the Stage while the marshals have to extricate you and flags are waved to let the others know you've well and truly boobed—again!

Remember, you are not in the Grand Prix Hyde Park Corner, and therefore try to circulate a track at about 9/10ths of your max. You then have that extra tenth just when it's called for—i.e. when you need to pull back some forestry misfortunes that have occurred earlier in a rally. The extra little bit is useful to get out of trouble as well as being on hand to pass a rival in front of the pits— the ultimate deterrent without a doubt, and guaranteed to demoralise any opposition.

Another point is to avoid actually passing someone on a corner if it means that the line that you have to use is in fact slower as a result of your heroics.

Braking

When braking on a race circuit or on any tarmac, where you are being pushed by your navigator to the limit because he's worried about the time, use the maximum braking pressure without actually locking up the wheels. You must toe-heel your way down the box under braking,

made easier with a nice set of close-ratio cogs, and try to keep the car really steady without any drama. If you want to really push things, use a harder brake pedal pressure, leave the braking point until a little later— and miss out a gear every now and then on the way down the box. You will then have shortened the braking distance. You can afford to really stamp on the anchors if you've got a nice cooling down brake-free piece of motoring straight after the bend that you're anchoring up for. Don't rely on the engine for any braking effect if you are in a hurry. The object of the engine on a swiftly driven rally car is to go go go. It can be used also to assist any braking on the main brakes. A trailing throttle and an attendant change-down when required is only useful as a steadying aid to stabilise the car prior to the next clog on and off, after the cause for speed reduction has been passed by safely.

Try to forget the speed you are going, what matters is the time you put up over the test. Rev readings are of much more import than bothering to glance at the speedo, you shouldn't have the time!

On a repeat section of road, as on a race track, you can start taking several corners as a series and not take each corner in its own right. After all, at every track, you can take one corner at maximum and find yourself at entirely the wrong position for the ensuing one—and at the wrong speed to do anything about it. If there are several bends before a straightaway, concentrate on achieving the perfect corner on the last one before the straight, so you enter the straight at the highest possible speed. You may have to sacrifice cornering speeds on the corners in the middle of a series to achieve this idealistic state of affairs. Always aim for achieving a rhythm around a track, you want to save all the frights for the woods.

If you have a certain number of laps to do at a circuit and no more, then it's absolutely vital to count the laps. Now it's virtually impossible to count them up yourself whilst you're howling round—especially as invariably you are in a pretty ropey state at this end of the rally, and not fit enough to count up to ten—let alone remember things. Besides, you want to concentrate on the time you are putting up each lap. So get a lap counter singalling from the pit area, or tear off bits of pre-stuck-on tape from the dash each time you pass the completed lap point. Naturally, if it's one of those tests where the poor old navi has to come too, then keep him awake by yelling "How many more laps?", or something more suitable as befits an occasion of strain.

Stage technique

I am often asked at Motor Club nights how I drive on special stages. Well I've attempted to work out exactly what happens . . . and don't blame me if you come unstuck trying out any of the advice in real life action—and disaster!

I merrily motor along the woodland tracks with one hand on the wheel and—on the old Imp—with one on my cunning hand-brake which has an extra handle welded onto it, so that it falls more easily to hand and doesn't lock on. I then brace myself against the door and sit sideways in my bucket seat without belts—but this is only a personal view. I just don't want to get trapped in a car in a shunt and reckon I've a better chance at surviving without being belted in. Natu-

rally I am ignoring the statistics but it's my opinion.

I place my right hand at the top of the steering wheel, which is incidentally a padded leather rimmed one with thumb spats covering the spokes.

On the loose, I try to keep the car in a continuous slide—but always a controllable one. It's quite definitely slower in certain parts of the woods as the resultant side-slipping does tend to scrub off some of the speed and sap the power, but it's so much safer. I hardly ever use the foot brakes. I keep the motor screaming at the top end of the power band for most of the time, so I'm an all gears and throttle man. Even when pressing on a bit, I always use the handbrake to ease the car round. The above activity is based on what I do in the Imp and differs slightly for other cars that I drive.

On a front-engined car like the Marathon Hunter, the same technique would be used by yours truly. On any similar layout machine, I still drive with one hand at the top of the wheel. But I lay off the handbrake, as with a car of that sort of weight and size this just isn't on. A front-engined rear-wheel drive car must be set up properly for a bend. You must judge where you are going to slide it to, unless you enjoy modifying the panels as well as most of the scenery. On a big weight car, and on a car of this type, I use the brakes far more too, before the corner, except when things tighten up very suddenly. Then I hammer them on at the same time as the power, to try and slow the car up, without understeering off the track or indeed powering the tail off into the undergrowth.

I started rallying in a Mini and worked my way through plenty until

I had a pretty potent 1293 Group anything S bomb. I used the same technique as with the Imp, the throttle on my Mini bringing the back into line or throwing it out as required. Left foot braking and bags of the old handbrake works a treat, there is possibly no more responsive bolide to the drastic whims and panics of a driver. The Mini can be spun like a top on a postage stamp, without rolling over too, which is always guaranteed to impress even the most cynical forestry gnome as he flees into the undergrowth at the sight of incredible antics.

Left foot braking may seem a bit of a mystery to many. One immediately conjures up visions of Timo, Rauno or Hannu on the pedals doing a dance fantastic. The whole basic principle is of course to slow the car down without having wheels lock up or have the car deviate violently from the track. It is in fact a sort of Maxaret braking—but with the feet. The Swedish experts don't think about what they are doing, it comes naturally just like skiing does to an infant in the Alps. The fine art is to balance the brakes against the throttle as you set the car up in the yaw required. It is hard on brakes if you are like Timo and use this technique at all times on the loose, but is best used by GB tyros to get yourself out of a whole lot of trouble . . . i.e. to reduce your speed suddenly without too much drama. But please practise the technique at an Autocross or on an icy deserted airfield first and don't go and try your new fangled Swedish cunning out on the local housing estate, not only will you incite the natives to much wrath, but you'll find straightening out all those wheels mighty pricey.

Their other ploy is to throw the car the wrong way on the loose before a bend. If you find, like I did, that this starts to happen as a natural slalom reaction then you're halfway there. All this does is to get the car braking down the speed more safely and effectively, as well as helping to swing the car round on its steering wheels under power. It's all very strange, but it really does work, and all the fast ones use the two techniques of throwing the car the wrong way and left foot braking to varying degrees of prowess and abandon.

Accidents

The other point to prepare yourself for is the avoidance of Le Grand Accident. Accidents over the edge or into the branches, or even both, do happen. You've got to face up to this eventuality. But the experts have cultivated their driving to such an extent that they can avoid going straight on at a panic T, they can get round an almost impossible corner without losing too much paint or hair, and they can spin the car to a stop in a length or two. If you see yourself aiming for a bump, don't for heavens sake slam the anchors on . . . and wait for the bang. The accidents always take so much longer this way. Try to get round, invariably you will do . . . even if you bounce off a bank, slither along in a ditch or scare yourself silly. The oldest novice error in the rally game is to brake like hell and cannon off without even a trace of cornering. If you really are going too fast, then use the brakes by all means, but try to use the left foot and hold the power against the pad pressure to avoid a lock-up. Here again the more practice you can get the safer you will become.

In your manoeuvres, always study yumps carefully. If you are clever, you'll be able to use the yumps to maximum effect. The car can be pushed from one side of the track to another. It can be made to hop, skip or jump—but always drive the yumps. Don't get caught off your guard by them.

Don't larrup the power on going into a yump—unless it's just a little one. Certainly avoid putting lots of revs through the drive when the car is in the air. Try to drive with the undulations so that you are always in control. Never brake the nose down into a hump. If you don't bash the sump to bits you'll put the steering out on the way in . . . and then there's that shell braking lurch as the car flumps down in a heap on the other side whilst you and your crewman are picking yourselves out of the headlining. Brake before the hump if it's seen, easy over it, and as you land power it along until the next one. Try to conserve the transmission train as much as you can . . . always remember doughnuts are not infallible. If you don't see the yump, and it catches you unawares, don't panic, don't lift off too violently, don't weave—just hover and keep treddling. It sounds very difficult but practice and knowing your motor will perfect the painless and successful negotiation of yumping in the woods. If you don't learn to take them pretty fast, your times will get very slow indeed. When you get more confidence, you should be able to take even the most fearsome humpery with great aplomb, and not too much damage—even to teeth and the like !

Night driving

Driving like crazy at night is just the same really—that is if you've got the correct lamps set up properly. But whether you have all fogs or all spots, or a combination of any of these plug/or extra driving lamps is a personal matter. Different set-ups suit different drivers.

In fog, which incidentally I dislike intensely—unlike Roy Fidler who always leaves everyone else standing when the fog is at its thickest— I follow the left-hand side of the road with my scanners on the road section, and concentrate on the banks to the left or the trees for that matter on the stages. I leave the instrument lights on, and run on dipped ordinary headlights—not QI as I personally find them too bright when the fog is thick. I don't have special fog lights and keep my spots off. After all, you only have to take a look round a major rally start to see the many interpretations of lighting that are currently being employed by the lads to see that it's a subject entirely variable. Some prefer yellow light too, but most stick to white.

In fog some drivers prefer to get as close to the screen as possible, and some like to dim out their instrument lights or turn them off altogether.

The best tip I can possibly pass on is to watch very closely the techniques employed by the present day experts—and profit by their mistakes. Learn safely, build up your speeds, never take chances, build up confidence in your ability to react subconsciously. When it all comes naturally, and only then, have a real go. You will come unstuck occasionally, the car will break more often, and you will spend a great deal of time and money. But if you're really hooked, you will go on and win awards. Then it'll seem really worthwhile.

As far as getting the first idea of what the sport is all about, try to get a ride in the back of a car on a smaller event, so that you become "au fait" with all the rally jargon. I got my grounding in rallying by sitting in the back—very instructive. For those without such an opportunity, learn by marshalling. Also for the thrills of driving on the limit on the loose, have a go at Autocross. This is still a relatively cheap and controlled way of getting to know your motor, and getting to know how to handle it around the course markers as well as the other competitors. My first season at Autocross taught me a great deal.

The Ex-Works Twin-Cam Escort of Sclater and Holmes on the Quantock stage of the 69 RAC Rally.

Roy Fidler and John Sprinzel enter Radnor Forest stage of the '69 RAC Rally. The car is a Datsun 1600 SSS.

A service car—the subject of some over enthusiasm in the driving department.

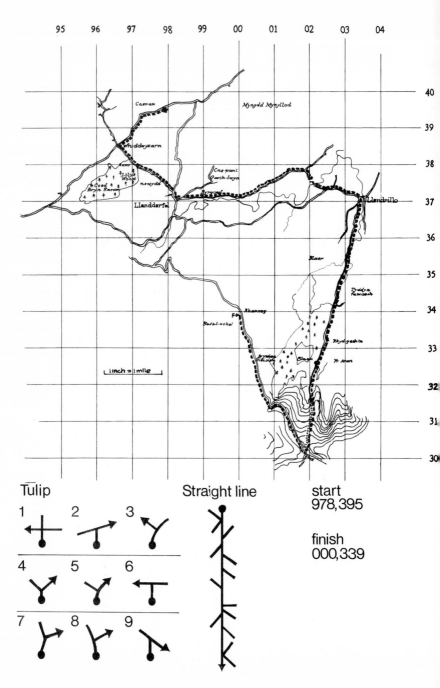

Tulip

1 2 3

4 5 6

7 8 9

Straight line

start
978,395

finish
000,339

70

chapter 10

THE NAVIGATOR

LET'S now consider the lot of those who have to sit beside he who pedals every rallying device—the learned sack of spuds, navigator, or, as they often prefer to be called—the co-driver. This very necessary human ingredient to every rally team is definitely one which needs much practice before the rewards of a well prepared car/talented driver combination can ever be reaped.

It's a very difficult job and I cannot emphasise enough here two things. Firstly, nobody, however keen, can necessarily achieve any distinction, or even mere proficiency straight-away. It's something that if you are going to be any good at, you'll show your form fairly quickly, and something at which constant practice is far more vital than at any part of rallying.

No training sessions

Secondly, if you've spent a great deal of hard earned bread developing yourself and car to the sort of speed that will be necessary to win awards on rallies, then you can ill afford to go rallying by giving a training exercise for a greenhorn—however keen on making the grade he or she may be.

An awful lot of guff is churned out by some of the text books, already written on rallying, of how two mad keen types can stick a few lamps onto the front of their grunge box and achieve instant success, or even mix it with the middlefield men, on sheer enthusiasm. The training bit is the next most difficult thing about navigating or co-driving. It's difficult to learn, because, let's face it, few outfits can afford to train you.

I started rallying as a navigator, and so can at least say that I appreciate the problems from the other side of the cockpit. But in the days of my slot reading, navigation was mainly of the bend reading/map reference plotting sort only. This sort of navigation is still very much part of the GB club rally scene, and should be considered separately from "special stage" co-driving. I propose now to discuss the skill of the latter school of activity, as it's more akin to the way all rallying is going to go in the future, and is of course what international rallies at home and abroad are all about.

Naturally enough, it's a tremendous advantage to graduate from the plot and bash herd as a top bod, for then you'll at least be a basically proficient navigator/map reader, as well as being thoroughly versed in the arts of crewmanship, which will have been collated through many club rally miles.

Let's deal with the qualities that need to be prevalent—or cultivated until they are an inherent part—in every co-driver's performance. Many of these qualities naturally apply to the map reading club rally navigator as well. At a later stage, I shall discuss the very specialised techniques that would need to be employed by navigators—but this is more rally navigation, as much as anything else. It goes without saying that the following basic qualities are directed at, and are obligatory for, all who wish to do well in rally co-driving.

Sitting beside one's man, whilst a quick stage time is being clocked, is not for the faint hearted. So one of the prime necessities for the aspiring co-pilot is to have very good unshakeable nerves. Whatever happens, he must be the very last person to get into a flap. It also helps to have the utmost confidence in the driver, who in any analysis should be trying his darndest to stay on the road, and should with luck be blessed with some slight tendencies towards self-preservation. As well as having confidence in the driver, it's mighty important for a co-driver to be confident in his own ability at coping with anything, and indeed doing his job properly.

A strong stomach helps, but it's quite usual, and is indeed a good plan, to take some anti-seasickness/travel sickness pills. Naturally, these ought to be tried out first, in case they induce drowsiness or double vision. Many of the best navigators are on the pill you see . . . such dedication!

Good eyesight is a boon, but in any case, every co-driver should ensure that he can at least see maps —and read them—or instructions accurately, even when the car is being pounded over the severest undulations. Instruments are difficult enough to read anyway in a moving car at night. But the basic requirement remains for co-drivers to be able to be accurate at spot visual checks of a trip meter's reading and a route instruction in a road book. So focus and accuracy, plus the ability of being able to peer at maps for hours with fascination and interest, rather than fatigue, are essential items on the job specification.

Physical condition

As days on end have to be part of the job's routine, it's pretty important for a crewman to be physically and mentally in A1 condition. So co-drivers ought to keep fit deliberately. This can entail some tremendously admirable domestic and alcoholic sacrifices. But remember when you too mount the winner's rostrum, it will all have seemed worthwhile after all. All sorts of taxing tasks occur in the course of a rally, and it's therefore as well to be equipped to cope with them. A car may fall off its jack and pin somebody underneath who was working on it. A car may need to be pushed out of a ditch alone by the co-driver unaided. An icy hill may need to be crossed by push power. The road may be blocked by a spun and crunched previous competitor, so some pretty rapid heaving may be required. It's tiring enough anyway, if nothing goes wrong with a car, so fitness cannot be over-emphasised.

It's all very well being Charles Atlas once, or maybe twice, but a co-driver's stamina to keep at it, when being taxed to the full, is also vital. It's the ability of maintaining this pressure without let-up that sorts the men out from the boys. Again stamina stems from a crewman's general fitness state.

The natural skills of navigation are common sense, as is the basic awareness of direction sense. The only instrumentation that needs to be understood is the Speedpilot or Tripmaster. Appreciation of distances is important without having to depend on a tripmaster, as invariably, at the most crucial point of an event, the speedometer drive cable, off which a Halda is driven, breaks. So much of navigation is merely common sense, practice, plus forward planning.

A co-driver is also the office manager. He must know everything about everything. He has to know all that is going on, both inside and outside the car. He has to watch fuel levels and decide where the car should be filled up and where it's OK to travel light on fuel. He has to know the regulations—and all the loopholes too. Neatness in writing and maintaining all those reams of paperwork, that seems to be a part of rallying all over the world, is very much a part of his job. He must have an orderly mind, which can easily adapt to cope with the latest unrehearsed problem to solve.

It's an asset for a co-driver to have a good mechanical sense, so he at least knows how a car is screwed together, as well as how to repair busted things on the roadside. It may be necessary for him to leap into the car and direct the driver through a maze of roads in a flash, whilst at the same time doing up the safety belt. There will be times when there will be no service crews around to patch things up. It's at times like this, that a proficient co-driver will be the asset that a competitive driver/car combination deserves— and indeed, these days, expects.

The co-driver has to be in charge of the ship. He must therefore master even the most awkward driver. If he doesn't direct the car's progress, the team will not be efficient military style. This may sound as if I reckon that co-drivers all ought to be mini-Hitlers devoid of a sense of humour. Well, all I'm saying is, yes—the sport has to be first and foremost sport, but never forget that a rally crew thrashing through the night down a tricky road is a serious business, with quite a risk on the cards. It has to be taken seriously by both members of the crew. Leave the funnies until the next halt and concentrate. Concentration is one of the most vital attributes for a good co-driver.

Information must be fed to the driver, and clearly too. It must also be the right information, the information that he needs to know. Drivers like to know how time is going. They like to know how far they have to treddle, and how fast they need to go. The driver's pace is up to the co-driver, looking ahead at the plan of the rally.

Navigating stages

To know what's coming is of course the main attribute. A co-driver will be able to tell this even on unseen "arrowed-only" stages, by having collected info from previous trips over the stage or selective. If it's on the map, he should have already added a detailed set of notes, so that he can call out the road to his driver. But I cannot emphasise enough here, that it's quite amazing how much quicker some drivers would go down a stage, if a co-driver shut up a little. Only call out the dodgy ones. After all these are the only ones that need to be treated with caution.

If there is some really rough stuff further down a track, tell the driver, so he can then adjust his pace accordingly, by going like merry hell prior to when he'll have to ease off to spare his car's underside. Pace notes are a must on anything of which the others are likely to have knowledge. These can only be built up in the co-driver's note book by sheer practice. The system used is best left to an individual co-driver, who can then understand his own abbreviations. It is essential, however, for a driver to understand what the notes or graded bends mean, in terms of what he can expect when the actual road presents itself before his very eyes. So all it needs is a little practice with a co-driver reading out notes for a piece of road, and then the driver telling the co-driver if the notes ought to be changed to suit his interpretation of the actual bit of road, having tried it.

The Turner seminar

Undoubtedly revered as Mr. Rallying, Stuart Turner, is now at the top of what has become, potentially anyway, the best international rally team ever assembled in the world. His brief at Fords has been simple. To win. It's going to cost Fords plenty too, but win they will.

But for Stuart Turner, there is thankfully more to rallying than just winning. Rallying has to have a future. It has to be accepted better and better, and by more and more people too. He has done plenty, and indeed is still doing, to make rallying more popular. His continuous publicity drives benefit Ford's rally team true, but also the very image of rallying itself is being effectively bolstered. Last year in the Turner promotional scheme was a co-drivers seminar, a "by-letter-of-application" happening which involved 26 hopefuls, who let themselves in for they knew not what. Some attended hoping that the vague challenge in a rally correspondence column, that was responsible for the seminar appearing at all, might lead to the ultimate works ride, others had come for purely rally education from the sport's most learned Don. As a whole, the course members soon treated the exercise as a useful opportunity to brush up their existing skills on this refresher course. One chap came along right out of the blue, having never even done a rally before, but just to satisfy some armchair curiosity.

However, the benefits that came from the course were two-way, and Stuart Turner used the occasion as an objective analysis as to what makes a co-driver and what's more a good one, tick. He laid on plenty of surprises for the seminaries starting off by assembling them at some unearthly hour at Stan Clark's garage up in Narborough, Leics, to be told to make their own way to Ford Competitions at Boreham for the next morning. At Boreham, it was a succession of lectures and aptitude tests, with some driving round pylons and running across the airfield to extract inner tubes from inflated knobblies fitted to Minilites. There was even a session with a psychoanalyst from the National Institute of Psychology. Films were shown to the lucky course members, so that they could have a go at writing out their own pace notes. Then top co-drivers, who also gave lectures, like Tony Ambrose, Jim Porter, John Davenport, and Mike Wood marked each members' attempts at note compilation.

If the course proved nothing else, it helped management and worker, in this case Turner plus his "pros" and the amateurs, to have a better understanding of the intricacies of professional co-driving and the way in which this job relates to the other aspects of the sport.

Some of the points raised by the lecturers are certainly worth repeating. Tony Ambrose reminded all of the dangers of relating notes on a recce to some items of scenery, particularly if those items of scenery might just be chopped down by a worthy local, or altered by a road works that might descend on the particular stretch of road, between the time when the notes were made and the actual passing of the rally. When putting natural hazards into notes, it's important to tie these hazards in, not only with the trip-meter's distance, but also the landscape, so that orientation after a long straight stretch of route is made more easy. Ambrose reckoned that a tape recorder is best for notes. And he summarised, by saying, that pace notes were not only useful to increase a crew's speed over a tricky section, but they made rallying a darn sight safer too. His concluding quote is a classic, and is worth repeating, "A co-driver can never win a rally, but he can always lose it!"

Stu McCrudden briefly told the course a few home truths about preparation, which is a good thing for any co-driver to be involved in, that is if he wants to finish. Stu did not approve of wasting money on flash accessories, but told any aspiring rallyist that they ought to spend their budget wisely on the priorities that matter. He went through all the usual cockpit safety gen, and said that on any rally car's preparation it was best to sacrifice power for torque. He declared that spacers were certainly out as far as rallying was concerned, and it was far better if the right width of wheel was chosen in the first place. He said that if a rally car looked right, in the works experience, invariably it was right. But this was not enough, it was important for any crew to keep their car up to scratch, and this involved painstaking maintenance between events.

An aptitude test of putting nuts and bolts of various sizes through a multi-holed piece of board proved to be a great test of fingers and thumbs, for which a time of 8 minutes was allowed. Turner cunningly stopped the test after only 7 minutes. No one spotted that the time was short, and so another lesson of checking organisers times was effectively demonstrated to the guinea pigs.

Pace notes

John Davenport told the seminar that the first pace notes were evolved by Stirling Moss and Dennis Jenkinson on the classic Mille Miglia race. Pace notes were perfected, under Turner, for International rallying at BMC. The International language of the pace notes is English. There is a basic system of notes common to all works teams. But there will be variations in abundance from driver to driver, and from co-driver to co-driver. He advised all co-drivers to put information from the route card or road book onto the map as a number one priority, that is if you have the time. Use a line on each side of the intended route, so that it's a corridor. Having the correct route on a map means that if the tripmeter failed at least it would be simply a case of map reading.

The code

Davenport developed his own system to its present highly professional stage with Vic Elford. Elford used to drive for Ford of course, before he moved to Porsche, and now on to Formula 1. Intercoms are a must for serious co-driver to driver communication. Davenport reckoned that the best way of calling out notes was to call the speed first, and then the direction of the bend next. "Flat" should be flat under any conditions. Then comes "Slight". However, "Fast" calls for a proper apex to be made by a driver or at least the alteration of his positioning to suit on the road. A "K" is a favourite amongst international rally men, meaning a 60 degree bend, so, a K can be K right or K left. Then comes a "Bad" right or "Bad" left, "Open Hairpin" and finally "Hairpin". The distance to the next note also has to be worked into the notes. The instructions if there is a space or there is at least a small straight between them, should be linked with a plus sign, but if they are on top of each other, the notes should be written next to each other with only a very slight gap. If there is a straight piece of road between the bends of a reasonable distance, it helps to write in, in yards, that distance. Then there is "B" for brow or "C" for crest. If a direction change is necessary at a "C", then it's "At C", then the bend instructions. Long or

"L" can be added before notes too. Often, it's helpful to slot in landmarks, where an arrow in the notes means leading into.

Then came a timed arithmetic test. A couple of examples of the sort of problems they had to work out, timed on the clock, were as follows: Time allowed 44 minutes—distance 39 kilometres—what is the average speed in kph? And, Combien font sept fois neuf fois trois? All very difficult, particularly when by this time they were all getting very tired.

A run through of all the various tyres that Goodyear supply to the Ford rally team was quite interesting. And this was followed by a practical demonstration of a tube change with only a rubber dolly hammer and a pair of tyre levers. Course members then had to carry this out for themselves, after a hearty run across the airfield to find a pair of tyre levers and the tyre on wheel from which to extract the tube. Then it was back across the airfield on wobbling feet over the line for more points to be assessed for the final order. After all a co-driver might have to get a tube out on his own.

Steve Poppleton gave a common sense thing from the Institute of Psychology. We couldn't really make head or tail of some of the answers, but apparently if you have what it takes to make a professional co-driver, then no problem. An example of a question was as follows: FIN SNIFF CUT SUCK XXX PETAL...?!!!

Once a Co-driver?

Ambrose told all that it was important for co-drivers to realise that the No. 1 driver was indeed the star and, in his experience, most co-drivers, Vic Elford excepted, stayed as co-drivers. He said that Marathon type events will mean that co-drivers will in fact do more driving. But, the driving technique of a successful co-driver must be such that the No. 1 gets as much sleep as he needs. It is essential to drive really smoothly, and not be worried about being overtaken. It helps to pre-prepare a piece of route. So when a co-driver has to take over the wheel, he shall have all his route made out on an illuminated postcard. This is so the co-driver doesn't have to rummage about in the road book, or keep peering at a map in between turning the interior light on and off. Ambrose reckoned that "wakey-wakey" pills were a safety essential, and should be taken. In his experience, the worst rally accidents invariably happened on straight roads, often fatal, and were quite obviously a case of people falling asleep at the wheel. However, the side effects of taking such pills should be watched most carefully. In some cases, extreme over-confidence or even loss of interest had been known to occur. He advocated regular co-driver/driver partnerships. And that it was vital for all co-drivers to spare the rally car as much as possible when they were driving, after all enough wear is bound to take place on the special stages and fearsome bits of the route. He concluded by saying that it was most important never to follow anyone else just for the sake of following them, after all, everyone makes mistakes, and it's all too easy to follow somebody blindly along a stretch of the route or rather not on the route for miles after mile and find oneself out of time as a result. Everyone makes mistakes, and so it's as well to make your own. When a co-driver is driving his driver, choosing his own pace and making his own navigational decisions is all a part of his trade.

Where a stage is unknown, the co-driver ought to try to jot down the interesting bits, if they've been given a tulip card on the line diagrams, so he then has a set of useful notes for the next time that that stage is used. If there are just arrows, he ought to read off the distance, so that the driver knows how far he has gone on the stage plus how far he has to go. As well as this trip reading exercise, it's as well to call out the arrows as the co-driver sees them—just in case the driver is pre-occupied with an instrument reading, or a mini skirted fab-piece on the stage side. We'll go into the preparation of pace notes as well as map navigating shortly.

Naturally the co-driver has to keep all the paperwork, do the accounts on who owes who what in the car— and keep an eye on the average being achieved; in short, a time keeper and a computer all in one. It's a far more exacting job than merely driving. Yet it's something that all drivers ought to have done at one time or the other in their formative rallying years.

Relief at the wheel

It also helps, if the co-driver can take over the driving on a part of an event when the driver can get some sleep. He therefore has to be able to keep up a good average without taking any risks—and conserving the car as well. Whilst driving, he also has to keep the car on route, so he has to be able to navigate at the same time. He therefore should be no mean driver too.

A co-driver must be able to make decisions rapidly—whilst under pressure. But above all, he has to be entirely logical.

After the day's concentrated lectures and tests, and a hearty cup of Ford Motor Co. soup, the night activities commenced for the course members. Their first task was to rush from Boreham under their own steam to the Excelsior Hotel, London Airport, to try to locate Hannu Mikkola, to buy him a drink ! Then it was on to Stonehenge—no, not to see the Druids, but to locate Chris Sclater. At this freak control a welding task was collected, which consisted of a couple of bits of metal. Then it was on to Gatwick to collect proof of a visit. And then on to Lydd Airport to find Jim Porter and his 3 litre Capri for a check in, and to hand over the welding completed—all this in the middle of the night ! Then back up from the depths of Kent to the wold of Essex and Boreham again, during which time the course members had to move their wheels round which had been marked previously. And then, absolutely dog tired, a set of Monte Carlo Rally regulations, which had been handed to them at Lydd had to be absorbed by the time they reached Boreham again for a post-breakfast questions and answers session. Phew, pretty tough, but then a co-driver's lot is mighty tough at times, and there was also a final order to be determined for the prize. All this sort of caper was to prove initiative, which is one of the most basic ingredients of being a successful co-driver.

This Turner happening was convincingly won by Club Rallyist Alex Jardine, 28-year-old Computer Programmer from Sidcup, Kent. His prize was to win a Monte Carlo Rally reconnaissance trip alongside Jim Porter. And who knows what then ? Second was Flt. Lt. B. Otridge, who rushed off to RAF Changi in Singapore straight after the course, with Rodney Spokes in third place.

The real value of such a do is difficult to appreciate immediately, certainly it's difficult to see any immediate concrete benefits, but, if the activities of Academy Turner on such a weekend did nothing else, at least they helped a few more folk along the way to having a more professional approach to what is after all rapidly becoming a highly sophisticated sport. After all, a little classroom exercise never did anyone any harm, now did it ?

chapter 11

CLUB RALLY NAVIGATION

BECOMING a competent club rally navigator needs many skills. But about the most important is undoubtedly experience. There is no easy way to the top. Most of today's aces started on local treasure hunt type events, and graduated slowly through closed club events and smaller Restricteds to the National and Restricted championship events that make up the MN series.

Let's have a look at the sort of gear that the club rally navigator should have around him. These comprise the following: the relevant maps, a romer, a supply of soft pencils, a pocket watch, map board—and the all important map magnifier. If events with selectives (road section timed to the second, of a demanding nature) or special stages are included in the event, then a stop watch and skid lid will be needed. Always check out the gear before you rush off on an event—it's so easy to slip up over maps in particular. One inch to the mile Ordnance Survey maps are used on GB club events, the regs for each event listing the map numbers that you'll be needing. Ensure that you obtain the very latest editions of these maps, as there is a definite advantage to be gained from having the benefit of the greater accuracy and more modern interpretation that the latest editions afford.

Added confidence can be gained from using marked maps as well. This means that the very important additional information about which white roads are goers (the term for negotiable or no), tricky bends and junctions, plus not-on-map hazards have been marked onto the map. The best person to obtain marked maps from is Stuart Gray, 1 Holts Close, Great Brickhill, Bletchley, Bucks. It is also well worthwhile to spend a little time before the event adding, with a felt pen or similar, a network of grid numbers over the map to supplement those on the borders. This can save valuable time when plotting the route, as you don't have to keep going to the edge of the map and follow the numbers along to the point which you're plotting. One more point to remember with maps is that after four or five rallies have been pencilled in—and subsequently erased

—the map becomes much harder to read clearly. So don't hesitate to replace worn maps with new ones. Also, if you buy flat unfolded ones, you can save a shilling a time over the folded cover variety. And every shilling counts in our sport!

I have tapped brains of somebody who's really au fait with the club rally navigating scene, Nigel Raeburn, who is one of the best MN type navigators, currently campaigning most weekends in Will Sparrow's successful Mini Cooper S.

A romer, for the greenhorn, is a small piece of plastic calibrated to enable you to accurately sub-divide by ten the one kilometre squares on the map, and so be able to accurately plot the six figure map references. How to plot a reference is all demonstrated on the map bottom and can always best be reiterated by the easily remembered ditty "Along the corridor—up the stairs". Once you know how to plot a reference, it's all a matter of building up plotting speed. Pencils, pocket watch and map board do not really need amplification, but a brief word on map magnifiers would perhaps be useful. It was only when Nigel started to go rallying with Will Sparrow, that he first used a decent sized magnifier powered from the car's power supply. For the previous seven years of his club rally career, he had somehow managed—as indeed many still today do—with a small battery-powered magnifier. But looking back, he doesn't know how he managed at all. Motto—obtain a magnifier or as the boys call them—"A Potty".

So now our budding navi. is properly equipped. Let's consider how he or she; after all what better reason for any male driver to run out of petrol, can unravel the organisers' instructions into a route, and then how to pass on that route to the driver in an effective manner. The commonest, simplest, and most popular means of defining the route is by map references, accompanied by directions of approach and/or departure for each point, given by points of the compass.

For example, "123456 approach NE, depart SW" means approach map reference 123456 from the north-east and depart to the south-west. On the more serious club rallies these days, the route card is issued about one hour before the actual motoring commences, so the navigator has time to plot the route and consult fellow navigators about any queries before the actual start. The navigator can then concentrate on keeping the car on the correct route, and calling out the bends to his driver. Once extensively used, but not so popular today is the "plot and bash" system when the route instructions are issued at various points on the route, and plotting has to be done on the move. There is quite an art in plotting references accurately, as well as deciding which tracks to select, and in which order, while you're being driven down a bumpy white road at 70 m.p.h. !

Tulip system

At the treasure hunt level of rallying, the number of ways organisers' cunning minds can devise to define the route are countless, but other fairly common techniques are the Tulip diagram and straight line diagram. The Tulip system—first used in the international rally of that name —uses a diagram for each junction, with a dot to indicate the direction of approach and an arrowhead the direction of departure. On one side of each aerial diagram of what the road looks like at the various junctions is a mileage reading to the tenth. So the junctions can be checked off against a trip as they appear in sight, or, what is more important, before the car arrives at them. This way, the driver is all ready for the next direction change. A straight line diagram shows the route straightened out into a straight line, with the junctions shown correctly to the left or right of the line. For example, a right turn at a crossroads will appear as passing two turnings at the same point on the left.

Timing

Timing is a topic which is very extensively covered in the regs for each event and the RAC's Blue Book,—the "Motor Sport Year Book and Fixture List". Every navigator should know the rallying sections of the Blue Book inside out. It helps to arm a navigator for another very important attribute of success—the protest and counter-protest. Not that this publication should ever endorse the use of the protest flippantly, or merely for the sake of protesting, but every navigator will only too quickly realise its use, as in so many cases it's responsible for results being turned round to alter the advantage of one competitor over another.

The term "Targa Timing" is one you're bound to come across sooner or later, so an explanation may be helpful. This is a system which was devised by that master navigator—John Brown. It was first used in the 1963 Targa Rusticana Rally, run by the Oxford University MDC. In this system, every time control has a clock, which has been set up so that, for example, car number 7 should

arrive at each control at 12.07 on the control clock if it is on time. Similarly, car number 75 should arrive at 01.15. The control marshals issue to each car a card bearing the control number and the time on the control clock. At any time, the marshals may only issue a card bearing a time which is actually on the control clock at that moment. A simple but most effective system, and one that is used on most of the bigger rallies today.

One aspect of timing which sometimes puzzles the beginner is how rallyists interpret the time when timing is "to the minute". When this applies, as it usually does on road rallies, the second hand, unless synchronised with the minute hand, is ignored, and as read by the minute hand it is, for example, 12.27 from 12.27 and zero seconds until 12.27 and 58 seconds, when it becomes on the next second 12.28. That is, timing to the preceding whole minute.

Responsibility

Now our navigator should have enough knowledge to allow him to set off from the starting line. His job is primarily to keep the driver on the correct route, and secondary tasks are to feed the driver with enough information to enable him to drive fast and safely, and to keep an eye on the time schedule. The greatest requirement for keeping to the correct route is concentration—and to concentrate, you must have confidence in the driver and his ability. It is essential not to mentally drive the car, and also to keep imagining that if only he were behind the wheel he would be losing so much less time. Naturally the navigator will be securely belted to his seat, so he won't have to look at the road in order to brace himself for coming corners and bends. He can keep his eyes on the map most of the time, with glances up occasionally to look for landmarks to keep himself orientated. With experience, he can obtain a tremendous amount of information from a one inch map, and feed his driver with a constant commentary on what the road will do next, which increases his confidence, speed and safety enormously.

It is as well, however, to have an agreement with your driver that the ultimate responsibility is his. So that if you call "fast right" and the road actually turns into a hairpin left, you can still claim it was his fault that you went off!

Pace notes

To give an idea of the amount of information about the road which can be fed to a driver, the following is how someone of Raeburn's calibre would read the road for a section of the '69 Gremlin Rally, on map 140, from a control at map reference 635468 leaving to the north-east to a control at reference 645½452½ approaching from the east: "GO! . . . straight 3 tenths . . . fast right . . . 2 tenths 45 right . . . 2 tenths straight . . . nearly 90 left . . . 3 tenths straight . . . T junction turn sharp right . . . fast left . . . fairly straight for 5 tenths— FAST . . . house on left . . . NOW/ slight left and right . . . short straight, before fork left onto white . . . NOW, TAKE IT . . . slight left . . . sweeping 45 right . . . nearly 90 left into fast ford . . . junction turn nearly 90 right . . . fast right . . . fast left . . . fast left . . . fast straight for 5 tenths . . . take a yellow turning on the right . . . NOW, TAKE IT . . . fairly straight 3 tenths to the control

. . . phew!".

Pace notes are creeping into club rallies these days for some of the better known roads, such as Abergwesyn and Epynt. These are used by some, but not all, of the successful crews.

Another job for the Navigator is to check that the marshals give the correct time on your cards or road book. Anyone can make a mistake, and so if there is any doubt at all, ask politely to see the clock, and you can then check the time yourself. If there are sections timed to the second, time them with your stopwatch. You can then check that there are no discrepancies between your time and the organisers'. At the end of the rally, the poor navigator's job is not over, for while the drivers catch up on their sleep, the navigator has to check the results to ensure that there are no errors.

Car sickness is a malady from which some navigators suffer, indeed most navigators feel a little bit queasy on occasions. Certainly concentrating on a map, while being driven quickly on twisty undulating roads, is very demanding on one's stomach. Try not to eat a cooked meal within an hour or so of the start of an event. It helps to have some windows open in the car. Antisickness pills may help, although many of the "Pro" navigators reckon that their effect is largely psychological. On a long night rally, most people are affected by fatigue, which lessens concentration. On the better rallies, there will be enough excitement and interest to keep you awake. Be careful not to chat away with your driver about topics other than the rally. This is the easiest way to miss a slot and lose time.

Those are big boulders for sump crunching—the Cowan, Malkin and Coyle Hunter in some of the typical Australian scenery.

*Don't always rely on the petrol gauge. This works Imp uses a notched stick.
It is much more reliable especially for the last drop.*

Extra lights are necessary, but they should be sturdily mounted to avoid wobble and detachment through vibration. Note the soldered snap connectors—so that each light can be individually replaced without a major rewire.

Over 30 cwt of winning Hunter goes swimming in the Brachina Gorge.

chapter 12
THE MARATHON

THE London to Sydney Marathon was the most extravagant motoring bonanza of the decade—all 10,000 miles of it. It cost everyone connected with it a great deal of money. The competition managers of Europe have now had time to review the emptiness of their tills, and have finally collected from the outback what was left of the lavishly-prepared rally cars, only to prepare all over again for the Daily Mirror's World Cup.

The star finishers on the Marathon had a whirlwind tour of shows and showrooms, while their crews kept busy attending fabulous "doos" and functions at such a rate that if they were not professional rallyists prior to their little trip to Australia they most certainly are now. Colin Malkin was a member of the winning Hunter's crew who had rocked the world's headlines so magnificently.

Colin's first rally drama occurred quite early on at Paris when he bust the escalator at the airport control. Quite incredibly, nothing really went wrong with the car during the rally. This was a convincing demonstration of the preparation prowess of

Des O'Dell's team of Rootes works mechanics at the Humber Road works in Coventry.

Recces proved to be invaluable—especially where there was a choice of routes between controls. Andrew and Colin had cleaned the southern route between Sivas and Erzincan, but they discovered one hill that might have given trouble if the weather deteriorated a day or so before the rally's passing. So they laid on a local recce man the day before the rally, and, as a result of his getting stuck on horror hill, the Hunter finally used the northern route which was a little longer.

Colin certainly witnessed at close quarters the baulking that some papers made copy with. It happened that there was a thirty-mile straight before several miles of corners prior to a control, the Hunter having notes for all the brows. But just before the bendery, at the very end of the straightaway, a Holden tanked past, pulling a much greater top speed. So for the next few miles, where the Hunter could have been considerably quicker, the British crew just had to sit behind having

87

all their daylight effectively blocked out by the Holden's wings. It just happened that the driver unintentionally used up all the road—very effectively too! This sort of thing unfortunately was rather common on the Marathon from all sides, indeed even service crews were dragged into the war at times. To British rallyists this sort of conduct just isn't done—but Marathon events are rather a unique rallying challenge.

Teheran to Kabul in 23 hours was quite a challenge. Rootes, Citroen and British Leyland used the southern route across the desert. But there were several ways to get from Teheran onto the desert road. The Hunter trio doubled back along the route through the control through the city again with a Chrysler-Teheran convoy to go via a much smoother run to the desert. It was of course just the right decision, for one of the Leyland Landcrabs burst a displacer on one of the alternative linking roads. The northern route, although much longer, was used by Fords as well as all the private owners.

Colin said that by far the worst part of thrashing across the desert was the shortage of petrol, that is if you were foolish enough to take this way without firstly organising convenient petrol dumps. Rootes had arranged for a local Ali-Shell to be waving his seventh veil at the roadside, so that the Hunter crew could home-in on the bushel under which he had stored the precious golden fluid. On one occasion, unfortunately, Ali slept—Marathon or no Marathon—so the dump was missed. Fortunately the Marcus Chambers strategy had taken such certainties into account, there being always enough in reserve to get the Hunter to the next point.

By the time No. 75 reached Bombay, the crowds had run out of flowers—but there were always stones instead! When the screen succumbed to one missile—the crew went through the most terrifying experiences of the event. Colin remains unsure to this day whether the mob wanted to know—or kill them. As for the highly publicised bandits of Afghanistan, they didn't have a chance to have a go at the boys, as every half-mile of the route was policed with soldiers.

At Bombay the Hunter had made such a good time that there were eight hours in hand, so the Des O'Dell Quartet, right by the S.S. Chusan's quayside, gave the Hunter a most careful check which revealed nothing adrift at all. An extra lamp was strapped onto the middle of the anti-kangaroo bar for the Australian bit. Dunlop SP 44s were retained for the whole run apart from a change to 41s to cross the Nullabor Plain where high temperatures dictated a little less rubber and cooler tyre running temperatures. Due to the availability of higher octanes in Australia the cylinder head was changed over to the original H120 Rapier head.

Through lack of space many of the Chusan stories have to remain untold, and anyway the censor might not approve. But with "Gelignite" Jack Murray threatening to water ski off the stern in the middle of the Indian Ocean, and Colin's winning of a splendid trophy for Ballroom Greyhound Racing—there was sufficient variety until Perth.

Perth

All the chariots were steam-cleaned at Perth and checked over by the State police for illegal apparatus. Several cars had to remove their sirens to proceed from the trotting track in the order of general classification. Thus a real road race began. From this point it all happened with little opportunity to make up any time for a meal or other civilised necessities.

Andrew was number one. Brian's job was car manager, whilst Colin just had to drive at eight-tenths—which made quite a change to his customary Welsh pace. He had to keep Andrew fresh for the fast bits when they really needed to go. As a result Colin drove for hours on end and became completely exhausted, which all goes to show the wisdom in taking a three-man crew on such an ordeal.

Colin found it very difficult to sleep when he was off-duty in the car, being hurled about on the hairiest bits of rough something awful. From one side of Australia to the other he only just managed a couple of hours shut-eye and, for the first time in his long and very varied rally career, he was car-sick. The conditions were very tough on this trans-Australia run, with the intense heat, no let-up in the pace, difficult navigation with few guiding landmarks, and worst of all—the dust. They even had to tape up all the windows and most of the doors in an attempt at stopping it billowing through the cracks. The dust was such a menace that it made overtaking a real gamble, as well as hanging over the track for several minutes after a car had bumped its way through.

Across Australia the Hunter left the road four times. Firstly Colin hit a hole in the road when down-snicking from top overdrive to top, resulting in a five-to-six-times see-saw from one side of the road to the other, via the ditches, with one Coventry foot firmly braced on the loud pedal. The road and a straight course were regained without stopping.

Then with Andrew at the wheel, and a control in sight, a brake nipple at the back was knocked loose by rocks. Andrew put it sideways as he had lost the hydraulics. But with all the gear on the roof, and the Hunter being likely to roll over as a result, he prudently caned it straight into piles of sand. Although it sank well in, a Rootes service crew, with the help of some spectators from the control area, soon lifted the car back into the rally in a mere minute and a half. There was no damage—apart from their nerves, that is—and they made the control with just one minute to spare.

Then there was the hairy moment when the Scottish pair were asleep and Colin was at the helm—as he had been solidly for several hours. "Gradually", he said, "the dirt road melted into one muddy brown colour, which seemed to lose all its features as it went on, and on, into an endless straight." But the straight terminated at a T, and the Hunter landed up amongst the scrub balls. Needless to say, as Colin emerged from the bush back onto the road—everyone was awake.

The Hunter's last moment before the flag was when, on a tightish section, Andrew had had the car sideways for some time. Colin dozed in the back, and Brian was busy reading out his notes—then came a "write-off" tree right on line. Andrew luckily drove the car smartly off the road (to avoid certain and expensive timber contact) into a gulley. They were able to reverse back up again thanks to their limited slip diff. But they stuck firm a few feet from the edge. Lady Luck smiled on them again for Evan Green's 1800 sportingly towed them back into the rally.

At this stage in the event the survivors were all helping each other. But Des O'Dell had organised Pentastar service on the roadside, where it was more use to his car, than the other manufacturers who preferred roaring about overhead their mounts in fleets of planes, hoping to spot trouble!

Generalising, Colin said that it was not as rough as anyone said it would be. But every now and then there would be an almighty one-mile-an-hour hole. The surfaces in the outback were similar—only smoother—to most British forestry going, but more sandy and bone-hard. The Snowy Mountains were very like some of our own Border country stages.

The winning ingredients

After numerous Bagshot sorties the ultimate shell was made up from scratch. Plates were introduced at exactly the sort of points that might begin to suffer after incessant yumping for all those miles with all that weight on board. All the seams were brazed up so there was very little likelihood of the unit becoming unstitched. It was also important to construct a shell that could even survive the rigours of the occasional prang as well as being able to stand up to what staying on the road had to offer.

For crew protection a roll cage was securely introduced. With the other special equipment this brought the weight up to over 30 cwt. as against the standard spec's weight of 26 cwt. The roof had to support over 160 lbs. of essential gear,

including three wheels and tyres—plus a tin trunk of tools. Other spares were distributed evenly around the car, every available storage space was utilised—even inside the rear wings. A great deal of thought and simulated Marathon motoring was undertaken to determine which bits ought to be carried and which spares ought to be left in the stores.

At the front there was a maximum of five Lucas lights, plus a roof-mounted flame-thrower with a shield keeping all its beams facing the way ahead. This "Safari" type of light is very important in dusty undulating going, as the light sees over the top and effectively picks out hazards. Like virtually every other Marathon machine, the Hunter had a very substantial "Roo" bar which was strong enough to withstand banks and the like.

Petrol capacity was upped to 37 gallons, spread over more than one tank so that if there was a leak all would not be lost. The discs at the front and the drums at the back were the standard diameter, but were fitted with competition lining materials. The steering box was standard but with a higher ratio. H120 dampers were used at the front, and proved to have just the right level of absorption, whilst at the rear, a set of competition dampers were fitted. Tougher high-rate springs were used in view of the extra weight on board, and a 4.22 to 1 rear-axle ratio, plus limited-slip, coped with the traction and overall gearing. The gearbox was standard Hunter with overdrive, and the clutch was standard too. Export radiator straight out of the parts book and an oil cooler kept the fluids from boiling.

Licences, Fixtures List, Names and Addresses of Motor Club Secretaries
RAC Motor Sport Division,
31 Belgrave Square,
London S.W.1.   Tel.: 01-235 8601
Sumpguards and Underbody Protection Equipment
Supersport Engines Limited,
Church Road,
London W.3.   Tel.: 01-992 8838
Maps
Mr. Stuart Gray,
Rally Maps,
1 Holts Green,
Great Brickhill,
Bletchley, Bucks.
                Tel.: 052-526 420
Lights
Bosch Limited,
Rhodes Way,
Radlett Road,
Watford,
Herts.   Tel.: 92-44233
Cibie,
Britover (Continental) Ltd.,
387 Chapter Road,
London N.W.2. Tel.: 01-459 7256
Hella Automobile Equipment Ltd.,
Hanworth Lane,
Chertsey,

Surrey.   Tel.: 655-2291
Joseph Lucas Ltd.,
Competitions Sales Counter,
Great Oozells Street,
Birmingham.   Tel.: 021-643 8791
Wipac Group Sales Ltd.,
London Road,
Buckingham.   Tel.: 028-02 3031
Instruments
Smiths Industries Ltd.,
Sales and Service,
Oxgate Lane,
London N.W.2. Tel.: 01-452 8030
Yazaki,
Time Instrument Manufacturers Ltd.,
928 High Road,
Finchley,
London N.12.   Tel.: 01-445 0491
Seat Belts
Britax (London) Ltd.,
Proctor Works,
Chertsey Road,
Byfleet,
Surrey.   Tel.: 29-43141
Kangol Magnet Ltd.,
Kangol House,
Fitzroy Square,
London W.1.   Tel.: 01-636 8468
Trip Meters
Gemini Trip Meters,
G. A. Stanley Palmer Ltd.,

Elmbridge Works,
Island Farm Avenue,
West Molesey Trading Estate,
East Molesey,
Surrey.   Tel.: 01-979 7254
Halda Ltd.,
4 Brandon Road,
York Way,
London N.7.   Tel.: 01-607 1207

Carburetters
S.U. Carburetter Co.,
Wood Lane,
Erdington,
Birmingham.   Tel.: 021-373 7371
The Zenith Carburetter Co. Ltd.,
Honeypot Lane,
Stanmore,
Middlesex.   Tel.: 01-907 4343
Webers,
Radbourne Accessories Ltd.,
8 Bramber Road,
London W.14.   Tel.: 01-385 9167

Rally Equipment by Post
Les Leston Ltd.,
314 High Holborn,
London W.C.1. Tel.: 01-242 8655
Jay Motor Accessories Ltd.,
Highbury Street,
Lincoln Road,
Peterborough,
Northants.   Tel.: 0733-68247
Speedwell (Chesham) Ltd.,
260/300 Berkhampstead Road,
Chesham,
Bucks.   Tel.: 02-405 6961
Paddy Hopkirk Accessories,
Mill Accessory Group,
Two Counties Mill,
Eaton Bray,
Bedfordshire. Tel.: Eaton Bray 611
Supersport Engines Ltd.,
Church Road,
London W.3.   Tel.: 01-992 8838
Tudor Accessories Ltd.,
Beaconsfield Road,
Hayes,
Middlesex.   Tel.: 01-573 0442

Manufacturers Tuning
British Leyland Motor Cor.,
Special Tuning,
MG Works,
Abingdon,
Berks.   Tel.: Abingdon 251
Ford Motor Co.,
Performance Centre,
Boreham,
Essex.   Tel.: 024-528 661
Rootes Motors Ltd.,
Customer Tuning,
Gate 5,
Humber Works,
Humber Road,
Stoke,
Coventry.   Tel.: 0203-54034

Rally Car Preparers
AVS,
132 Smithdown Road,
Liverpool 15. Tel.: 051-733 7738
Allard Motor Co.,
51 Upper Richmond Road,
Putney,
London S.W.15. Tel.: 01-874 2333
British Vita Co. Ltd.,
Middleton,
Manchester M24 2DB
               Tel.: 061-643 4301
Broadspeed Ltd.,
101 Stratford Road,
Birmingham 11.
               Tel.: 021-772 0639
Brundle Tune,
Fox's Lane,
West Lynn,
Kings Lynn,
Norfolk.   Tel.: 0553-2910/2413
Clarke and Simpson,
49 Sloane Square,
London S.W.1. Tel.: 01-730 0436
Coburn Improvements,
7a Netherhall Gardens,
London N.W.3. Tel.: 01-435 6743
David Hirons,
The Cottage,
School Lane,

Rowington,
Nr. Lapworth,
Warwicks.   Tel.: 05643-2120
David Wood Engineering,
22 Queensgate Place Mews,
London S.W.7.   Tel.: 01-584 3552
Ian Walker Racing,
236 Woodhouse Road,
London N.12.   Tel.: 01-368 6281
Janspeed,
Southampton Road,
Salisbury,
Wilts.   Tel.: 0722-22002
John Heppenstall,
Trinity Garage,
Bradford Road,
Nr. Leeds,
Yorks.   Tel.: 09244-4523
Lynton Racing,
Fortis Green,

London N.2.   Tel.: 01-883 4036
Perdal Developments,
Wingrove Motor Co. Ltd.,
Westgate Road,
Newcastle upon Tyne,
NE4 9HD.   Tel.: 0632-33874
Race Proved,
177 Uxbridge Road,
Hanwell,
London W.7.   Tel.: 01-579 0991
Stan Clarke Cars,
Narborough,
Leicester.   Tel.: 053729 3638
Supersport Engines Ltd.,
Church Road,
London W.3.   Tel.: 01-992 8838
J. C. Withers (Winsford) Ltd.,
Smokehall Lane,
Winsford,
Cheshire.   Tel.: 060-681 3866

WIRING DIAGRAMS

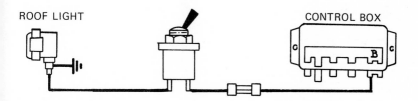

Navigator's roof light.

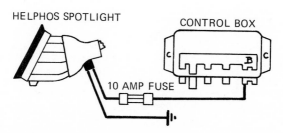

Helphos signpost spot light.

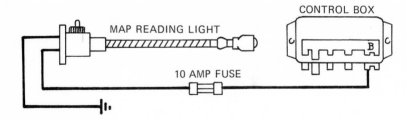

Map reading light. (Butlers)

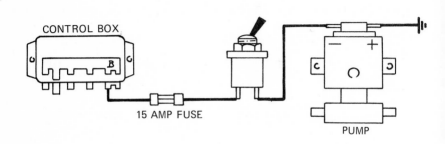

Electric windscreen washers (Waso)

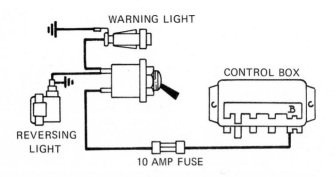

Manual control reversing light. Separate warning light.

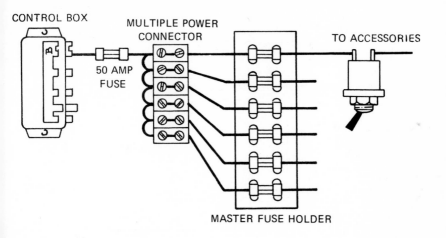

Master power and fuse control mounted inside cockpit.

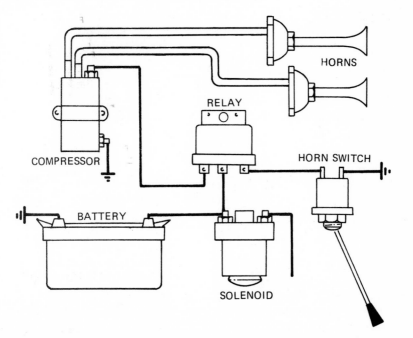

Maserati air horns.

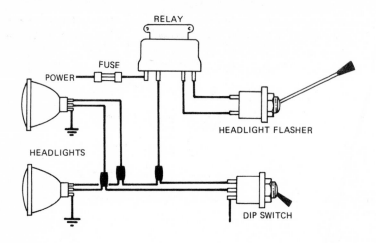

RELAY

FUSE

POWER

HEADLIGHT FLASHER

HEADLIGHTS

DIP SWITCH

Headlight flasher with relay in circuit.

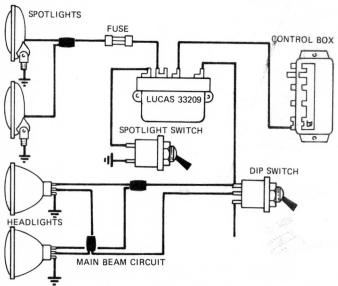

SPOTLIGHTS

FUSE

CONTROL BOX

LUCAS 33209

SPOTLIGHT SWITCH

DIP SWITCH

HEADLIGHTS

MAIN BEAM CIRCUIT

Two spot lights and relay. Operation of dip control cuts out spots and changes head lights from beam to dip. Cable for spot light connection is 28/012.

THE
PERFORMANCE
PAPERBACKS

INTERAUTO

A NEW SERIES
of
AUTO ENGINEERING
REFERENCE BOOKS

The following pages present to you some of the
current SpeedSport and Interauto books for the
motoring enthusiast, the automobile technician
and the motorist.

Motorsport

HOW TO START MOTOR RACING. Wally Hall. 011.9. £ 1.00

The author has had considerable club racing success and has passed on most of the vast experience he has gained. Ideal for anyone at all interested in beginning.

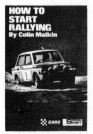

HOW TO START RALLYING. Colin Malkin. 024.0. £ 1.00

This famous rally driver takes the reader through all the mystiques of rally preparation. Car selection, suitability and setting up. Bodywork, lights, driving and navigation are some of the subjects dealt with. Colin co-drove the winning London to Sydney Marathon car.

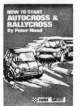

HOW TO START AUTOCROSS AND RALLYCROSS. Peter Noad. 033.X. 80p

Like the rest of the 'How to Start' series but for the increasingly popular sport of autocross/rallycross. Like the other authors Peter Noad is an experienced and successful campaigner.

TOUCH WOOD. Duncan Hamilton. 042.9. £ 1.50

Paperback   25 b/w illustrations

We feel that we have found a great book in **TOUCH WOOD** and have re-issued it as the first title in our reprint series of motor racing classics. Duncan Hamilton was typical of the enthusiastic amateur who went racing for the sheer hell of it. He drove many makes of car to their limit, mostly Jaguars, utterly indifferent to his own safety and surviving many spectacular accidents. He won Le Mans at over 100 mph suffering from a monumental hangover, crashed an aeroplane, was torpedoed twice and helped to put England back on the motor racing map. His autobiography is a marvellous colourful story and has been out of print for a long time.

HOW TO START PRODUCTION MOTOR CYCLE RACING   Ray Knight   030.5   £ 1.00
Ray Knight
Ray Knight is a journalist with 10 years racing, a TT win and lap record to his credit. He passes all his experience to the enthusiast. 'A good guide to success.'

THE *BARRY LEE* BOOK OF HOT ROD RACING   062.3   £ 1.00

Barry Lee revolutionised Hot Rod Racing in 1970 and in 1971 became British Champion, as well as making successful forays to Denmark and South Africa. In his book Barry Lee shows how he built his Escort, what it's like in a hot rod race, where and when hot rod racing takes place - in fact he writes about everything that an intending competitor, a hot rod fan or spectator will want to know.

Marque tuning guides

TUNING THE MINI. Clive Trickey   001.0. *£ 1.00*
The Mini Tuners' Bible; universally recognised as the most authoritative book on the subject. The most popular marque tuning book to be published.

MORE MINI TUNING. Clive Trickey   000.3. *£ 1.00*
New! The second edition of the companion volume to **'Tuning the Mini'.** Updated with much more information on valve gear, carbs, camshafts and gearboxes.

TUNING STANDARD TRIUMPHS up to 1300 cc.   012.7. 50p
Richard Hudson-Evans
Essential reading for Herald, Spitfire, 1300, Standard 8 and 10 owners. Full tuning information.

TUNING STANDARD TRIUMPHS over 1300 cc.   029.1. £1.60p
David Vizard
The tuning stages for Vitesses, GT6, TRs and all 2000 units from stage 1 to full race.

TUNING VOLKSWAGENS. Peter Noad   026.7. *£ 1.00*
An expert guide to the race and rally preparations of VWs; it covers the various types of car and their development and competition history. Includes a section on Beach Buggies.

TUNING ESCORTS AND CAPRIS. David Vizard   009.7. *£ 1.00*
The technical editor of **'Cars and Car Conversions'** explains engine and chassis tuning procedures for both road and track.

TUNING ANGLIAS AND CORTINAS.   003.8   80 p
This bestseller deals with engine and chassis tuning and details the early Classic and Capri, the V4 and Twin Cam power units.

TUNING TWIN CAM FORDS. David Vizard   007.0. £1.00
The stage-by-stage modifications for these engines, from 'warm' 1600s to full-race 1800s. Fully illustrated.

TUNING FOUR CYLINDER FORDS. Paul Davies.   059.3. £1.00.
A new edition of this very popular tuning bible for all four cylinder models from Anglia to Cortina MK III.

TUNING BMC SPORTS CARS. Mike Garton   004.6. 80p
The author, once a technical expert at British Leyland Special Tuning Department passes his wealth of experience on to the interested owner

TUNING IMPS. Willy Griffiths   052.6. 50p
The Imp is one of the most difficult cars to modify. The author lets out all the secrets on what can and cannot be done. **NEW 2nd Edition.**

TUNING VIVAS AND FIRENZAS Blydenstein & Coburn 064.X £ 1.00
Written by the country's leading experts, this is the first tuning book on these popular cars. It covers all aspects of tuning for both road and track.

TUNING V8 ENGINES. David Vizard   028.3. £1.50p
This book covers the principles involved for modifying a large selection of V8 engines— design trends, supercharging, assembly, part swapping, carburation etc.

TUNING SIDE VALVE FORDS. Bill Cooper   005.4. 80 p
This book covers the 100E engine fitted to early Ford Anglias and Prefects now finding their way into many youthful hands.

BUILDING AND RACING AN 850 MINI. Clive Trickey. 010.1. *£ 1.00*
Another winner from Clive Trickey who describes here the story of his own racing success in a step-by-step method that can be followed by the would-be racer.

Carburetter guides

TUNING SU CARBURETTERS.   017.8.   104 pages, 30 illus.   70p

The SU carburetter is fitted to all BLMC and many other cars and is often used for carburetter conversions to tuned cars. This book is a complete guide to their tuning, servicing and fitting, with recommended jets and full needle charts, both for the enthusiast and economy-minded motorist. Recommended by the Manufacturer. Covers carburetters fitted to Aston Martin, BLMC, Citroen, Daimler, Ford Conversions, Hillman Conversions, Jaguar, Jensen, MG, Renault, Rover, Triumph, Volvo, also suitable for HITACHI carburetters.

WEBER CARBURETTERS. Vol.1 - Theory & Conversion Practice.   John Passini.   018.6.   70p

This book covers the setting-up, method of operation and servicing on one of the finest carburetters available for high performance engines. Written by an acknowledged specialist on these carbs. Suitable in conjunction with Vol.2 for Mini, Ford, Volvo, VW's, Alfa Romeo, BMW, MG, Fiat, Simca, Peugeot and Lancia models.

TUNING STROMBERG CARBU-RETTERS.   006.2.   70p

A similar volume to the SU carburetter book but for tuning the very popular Stromberg carburetter. Again recommended by the Manufacturer. Suitable for Aston Martin, Ford, Hillman, Humber, Jaguar, Sunbeam Triumph, Vauxhall.

WEBER CARBURETTERS Vol.2 - Tuning and Maintenance John Passini   060.7   70p

This is the companion volume to the very successful Weber Carbs book by the same author, which dealt with the Theory of how Webers worked and functioned only. John Passini has worked very closely with the factory to provide in this book all there is to know about Weber tuning and maintenance. Profusely illustrated and complete with needle, settings and application data tables.

**TUNING SOLEX CARBURETTERS   R.C. Pack   069.0
                                                                        70p**

This book deals with problems and major tuning characteristics of Solex carburetters, and shows how to obtain maximum power from the engine.

TUNING COMPANION SERIES

TUNING LUCAS IGNITION SYSTEMS   063.1   £1.00

This book examines each component in the Lucas ignition system
and explains how to test and check that it is functioning correctly.
Also dealt with are the special procedures and requirements of
systems on high performance engines, with setting up instructions,
trouble shooting hints and comprehensive data tables.

INTRODUCTION TO TUNING. 002.X. 50p
ENGINES AND TRANSMISSIONS. 013.5. 50p
SUSPENSIONS AND BRAKES. 027.5. 50p

Martyn Watkins has written a basic guide
to the tuning and modification of
production cars. These three volumes of the
TUNING COMPANION series are designed
to take the beginner through the theory
and then the practice stage by stage.
They should then lead him into the more
detailed work featured in the rest of the Motobook range.

AUTO ELECTRICS.   David Westgate.   014.3.   £1.00
A well illustrated and easily readable guide to the car's electrical system.
This book should be a standard work as it covers all aspects of this
complicated subject from batteries to ammeters.

CAR CUSTOMISING.   Paul Cockburn.   031.3.   90p
A new book on this increasingly popular form of car modification.
Paul Cockburn a brilliant young designer explains the ground work and
suggests many practical ideas.

MODIFYING PRODUCTION CYLINDER HEADS.
Clive Trickey.   008.9.   50p
Clive Trickey's famous basic guide to the modification of cylinder heads for
improved performance. A standard work which has become a best seller.

RACING ENGINE PREPARATION.   Clive Trickey.   015.1.   £1.00
Fully describes the conversion of mass-produced engines to full blown
racing units.

New edition Castrol Book of Car Care

SBN 902-587-005
This is the new edition of the ever popular Castrol Book of Car Care in a new format and at a new price.
Car Care' has been rewritten and considerably updated, with new drawings, diagrams and photographs. It now has a full-colour cover.
'Car Care' does exactly what its title suggests under the following chapter headings:
1. A Happy Partnership? 2. Servicing; 3. Bodywork; 4. Engine; 5. Transmission; 6. Brakes; 7. Suspension and Steering; 8. Tyres; 9. Electrics; 10. Breakdown Trouble-shooter; 11. Safety and Security; 12. Castrol at your Service.

25p

Castrol Book of Motor Cycle Care

a sister publication to the **'Castrol Book of Car Care'** describes the various parts of the machine tells what they are designed to do and suggests the best course of action for looking after them. Used intelligently it can save a lot of time, money and frustration.

Still very popular and a constant best seller.

25p

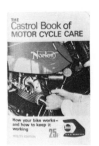

The Big Drive

THE BIG DRIVE.
Richard Hudson-Evans and Graham Robson.
032.1. 50p
The Book of the World Cup Rally, 1970.
The first behind-the-wheel view of the toughest rally ever—the car breaking London to Mexico Race.

HOW TO KEEP YOUR VW ALIVE. John Muir. £2.50
'A manual of step by step procedures for the complete idiot'
Softback, ring-bound, profusely illustrated

This brilliant book has been a huge success in America. It is written by an expert engineer who appreciates that complex technical procedures cannot be followed by the amateur mechanic. He explains how to look after a VW in simple language combined with a wry humour.
Basically a manual, but very different from any others. Extremely valuable even though unusual in approach. It is proving that the success in America was no flash in the pan.

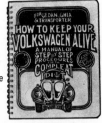

General Motoring

EMERGENCY SIGNS FOR MOTORISTS
ISBN: 0-903192-08-X Size: 11¾ '' x 8¼''

A book of easily-recognizable poster-size emergency signs which can save the user time and embarrassment by showing passing motorists that something is wrong. There is a sign appertaining to almost all situations — everything, in fact, from an 'ON TOW' notice to a hazard warning sign. Perhaps of most importance is the inclusion of signs relating directly to accident prevention and the need for medical assistance. A sign such as 'DOCTOR WANTED', displayed with a large cross, attracts immediate attention and is easily understood.

Officially approved by the Design Centre and featured on the television show **"Drive In"**, **EMERGENCY SIGNS FOR MOTORISTS** provides a service which is long overdue and which, as our roads grow ever more crowded, should become an essential item in the responsible driver's equipment. Remember: It will be worth more than its price when you need it!

INTERAUTO

Workshop Series

A range of books on important but much-neglected aspects of automotive technology for the engineer and mechanic.

PETROL FUEL INJECTION SYSTEMS
ISBN: 0-903192-20-9
Size: 8½" x 11"
380 pages Illustrated
One of the first books published containing detailed information on the construction and operation of most of the major petrol fuel injection systems available today. The opening section deals with the development of the first P.I. Systems, dating as far back as 1940. This is followed by descriptive information and technical data on various systems available on the

present day market. Finally, service information on a number of vehicles to which a P.I. System has been fitted.
With an abundance of clearly laid-out photographs, drawings and plans, and in the same large format as the other titles in the series, this book covers: AE BRICO, BOSCH(Mechanical and Electronic), KUGEL-FISHER, LUCAS & TECALEMIT in relation to the motor vehicles equipped with these systems.

ALTERNATOR SERVICE MANUAL
ISBN: 0-903192-28-4
Size: 8½" x 11"
250 pages Illustrated
This valuable publication for automotive electricians deals extensively with the testing and maintenance of Alternators and Regulators. Compiled from genuine manufacturers' service manuals.
CONTENTS: Alternator technology Bosch, Butec, CAV, Chrysler, Delco, Remy, Email, Fiat, Ford, Hitachi, Leece-Neville, Lucas, Mitsubishi, Motorola & Prestolite Application tables listing current vehicles and their standard alternators, for easy cross reference.

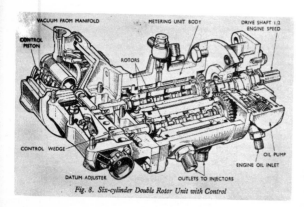

Fig. 8. Six-cylinder Double Rotor Unit with Control

Automatic Transmissions Setting & Test Data

Interauto Book Company Limited

Crypton Triangle (Transervice) Publications

AUTOMATIC TRANS-MISSION SETTING AND TEST DATA
ISBN: 0-903192-29-2
Size: 8½" x 11"
150 pages

Presented in a compact and easy-to-read format are the setting and testing procedures for the more popular automatic transmission systems in their adapted form for use in the majority of vehicles. Additionally, the book contains such information as pressure tables, shift speeds, the location of pressure take-off points, plus comprehensive fault diagnosis charts which enable the user to carry out checks and adjustments with speed and accuracy.

The subject of automatic transmission is a complex one. This publication does not purport to be a work-shop manual dealing with system overhaul and repair, but it will prove of great value to the service engineer involved in the final on-car setting and testing.

Transmission lists by vehicle make and model as cross-reference.

'Engine and Electrical Service' over 250 pages and 450 illustrations	£ 2.50
'Corrective Service' a new approach to fault finding that interprets all oscilloscope traces and meter indications	£ 2.50
'Diagnostic Wallchart' 40"x30", for quick reference, it shows all oscilloscope traces and related fault conditions	£ 2.50

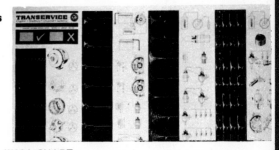

WALL CHART
40" x 30" three colour chart showing all oscilloscope traces. Ideal for checking "fault" conditions.

All your motoring books from ONE source

ALBION SCOTT LIMITED

are the sole distributors of all
SPEEDSPORT and INTERAUTO books.

Albion Scott also distribute a range of
over 1,000 other titles for the motor
vehicle.

We call them all MOTOBOOKS

Motobooks are over 1000 Workshop Manuals,
handbooks, tuning, maintenance and repair
nooks covering practically every car on the
road today. Books on racing, veteran cars,
motor sport, biographies, connoisseur books
and many more

We sell Motobooks

Where ever you see this sign   displayed, i.e. by good bookshops,
motor accessory shops or other retail outlets you can be sure that SpeedSport,
Interauto and the many other Motobooks distributed by us are for sale.

However, if you have difficulties in finding a suitable outlet you may order
directly from us using the form provided in this book.

HOW TO ORDER
Motobooks

Whenever you wish to purchase any of the listed books take this form to your Bookseller or Motorshop who will order the book for you. If this is not possible, mail the order form to us with your payment and we will send the required books to you by return.

Please observe the following instructions:

ORDERING
BOOKS   from
BY MAIL

ALBION SCOTT LTD.·
Bercourt House
51 York Road
Brentford Middx
TW8 OQP England

Identify required books on this form.
Mail complete form to us, with your remittance (either cheque, postal order or cash) to which you must add the postage as set out below.

Make sure that your
    NAME and ADDRESS is given in the space below.

Postage and Packing:

		UK	EUROPE	OVERSEAS
Book price to	£2.00	10p	15p	20p
	£3.00	15p	20p	25p
over	£3.00	20p	30p	40p

Dispatch by surface book mail only.

Name ....

Address ....

Special Instructions ....

Get your facts straight from a Motobook

SPECIAL TITLES FROM ALBION SCOTT

Qty.	Title	Price	Total
	SPEEDSPORT		
	Tuning SU Carburetters	70p	
	Tuning Weber, Vol.1	70p	
	Tuning Weber, Vol.2	70p	
	Tuning Stromberg Carbs.	70p	
	Tuning the Mini	£1.00	
	More Mini Tuning	£1.00	
	850 Mini	£1.00	
	Tuning Four Cyl. Fords	£1.00	
	Anglias and Cortinas	80p	
	Tuning Twin Cam Fords	£1.00	
	Tuning Side Valve Fords	80p	
	Escorts and Capris	£1.00	
	Tuning Vivas & Firenzas	£1.00	
	Tuning BMC Sports Cars	80p	
	Triumphs to 1300cc	50p	
	Tuning Triumphs over 1300cc	£1.00	
	Tuning the VW	£1.00	
	Tuning Imps	50p	
	Tuning V8 Engines	£1.50	
	How to Start Rallying	£1.00	
	Barry Lee Hot Rod	£1.00	
	HS Motor Racing	£1.00	
	How to Start Autocross	£1.00	
	Prod. Motorcy. Racing	£1.00	
	Introduction to Tuning	50p	
	Engines and Transm.	50p	
	Suspensions and Brakes	50p	
	Auto Electrics	£1.00	
	Lucas Ignition Systems	£1.00	
	Modif. Prod. Cy Heads	50p	
	Racing Engine Prep	£1.00	
	Car Customising	£1.00	
	High Speed Driving	£1.50	
	Cylinder Head Modific.	£1.50	
	Scramble	£1.00	
	Open Cockpit	£1.00	
	Hot Air Ballooning	£1.50	
	Touch Wood	£1.40	
	Keep Your VW Alive	£2.50	
	The Big Drive	50p	
	Castrol Bk of Car Care	25p	
	Motorcycle Care	25p	
	Qty TOTAL Price		

Qty.	Title	Price	Total
	INTERAUTO		
	Fault Diagnosis	95p	
	Interference Suppression	95p	
	Body and Paintwork	95p	
	Performance Testing	95p	
	Engine Testing	95p	
	Braking Systems	95p	
	Bosch Electrical Systems	95p	
	SU Carburetters	95p	
	Solex Carburetters	95p	
	Zenith Carburetters	95p	
	Stromberg Carburetters	95p	
	Weber Carburetters	95p	
	Caravans	95p	
	Alternator Manual	£2.50	
	Automatic Transm Data	£2.50	
	Petrol Fuel Injection	£3.80	
	CRYPTON		
	Engine and Electrical	£2.50	
	Corrective Service	£2.50	
	Diagnostic Wallchart	£2.50	
	WORKSHOP MANUALS		
	quote make, model & year	£2.00	
	HANDBOOKS		
	quote make, model & year	75p	
	Motorist Emerg Signs	75p	
	Motobook Catalogue	20p	
	Qty TOTAL Price		

NOTES.

Albion Scott Ltd., 51 York Rd., Brentford, Middlesex, TW8 OQP.